# the NATURE of KYOTO

WRITERS IN KYOTO **ANTHOLOGY 5**

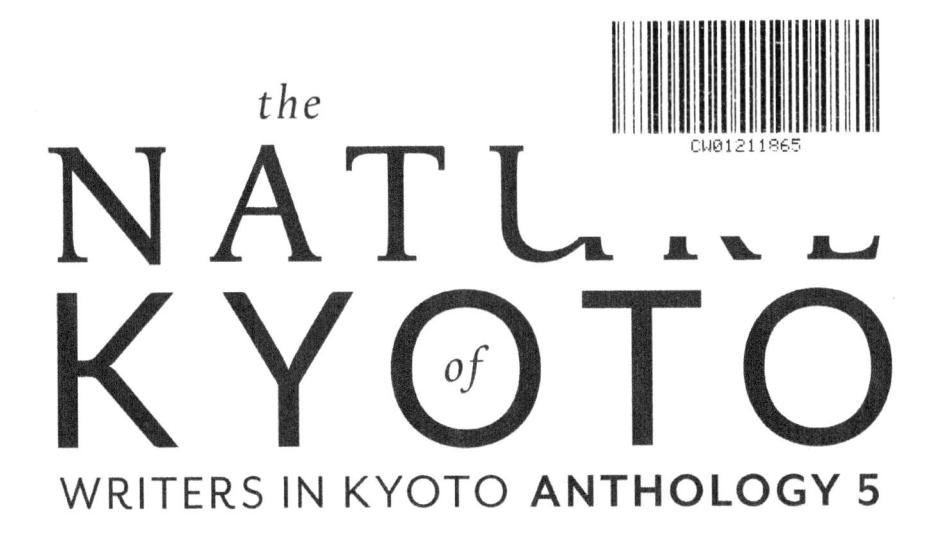

*foreword by* **PICO IYER**

*edited by*
**LISA TWARONITE SONE** & **ROBERT WEIS**

### CONTRIBUTORS

STEPHEN MANSFIELD · REBECCA OTOWA
JOHN EINARSEN · AMANDA HUGGINS
EVERETT KENNEDY BROWN · C. GREENSTREET
ELAINE LIES · EDWARD J. TAYLOR · FELICITY TILLACK
FERNANDO TORRES · HANS BRINCKMANN · HAMISH DOWNIE
IRIS REINBACHER · JANN WILLIAMS · JOHN DOUGILL
JULIAN HOLMES · KAREN LEE TAWARAYAMA
KEN RODGERS · KIRSTY KAWANO · LISA TWARONITE SONE
MALCOLM LEDGER · MARIA DANUCO · MAYUMI KAWAHARADA
PATRICK COLGAN · PRESTON KEIDO HOUSER · ROBERT WEIS
STEPHEN BENFEY · TETIANA KORCHUK
TINA DEBELLEGARDE · YUKI YAMAUCHI

DESIGN BY RICK ELIZAGA

# The Nature of Kyoto
## WRITERS IN KYOTO ANTHOLOGY 5

Edited by Lisa Twaronite Sone & Robert Weis
Foreword by Pico Iyer

Published in May 2023 by Writers in Kyoto
in the sublime season "of the fresh new green"

❋❋❋

For more information about
Writers in Kyoto (WiK), please visit
**www.writersinkyoto.com**

❋❋❋

Photographs by Anthology authors, Ed Levinson and stock images
Design by Rick Elizaga

COPYRIGHT
All works within are the intellectual property of
the individual writers and may not be reprinted, electronically
transmitted, or reproduced without their permission. The views
expressed by the authors are solely their own.

© 2023 Lisa Twaronite Sone & Robert Weis
All rights reserved. ISBN: 9798391482086

*With thanks to
John Dougill,
founder of Writers in Kyoto*

# Table of Contents

A Word from the Editors .................................................................. vi

Foreword: The Rain upon the Rooftops ........................................ viii
    Pico Iyer

Kyoto: Different Forms of Hypnosis ................................................ 1
    Stephen Mansfield

The Pocket Garden ............................................................................ 7
    Rebecca Otowa

Lotus 蓮 ............................................................................................ 14
    John Einarsen

Love on a Low Flame ..................................................................... 18
    Amanda Huggins

The Graveyard of Homyo-in ......................................................... 21
    Everett Kennedy Brown

Sudden Tsukimi .............................................................................. 28
    C. Greenstreet

For Love of the Octopus God ........................................................ 31
    Elaine Lies

Peeks on Danger .............................................................................. 37
    Edward J. Taylor

For the Visitors ................................................................................ 43
    Felicity Tillack

Nature is Trying to Kill You .......................................................... 49
    Fernando Torres

Restaurant Boer ............................................................................... 56
    Hans Brinckmann

The Nature of Kyoto: 1006 vs 2006 .............................................. 59
    Hamish Downie

The Revived Waterway ................................................................... 65
    Iris Reinbacher

Kyoto: City of Fire and Water ....................................................... 71
    Jann Williams

Vignettes, Interrupted ........................................................................ 79
 John Dougill
Food for Thought and for the Thoughtful ...................................... 87
 Julian Holmes
Recollections of Nature, Neighbors, and Nibbles ......................... 95
 Karen Lee Tawarayama
Local News ........................................................................................ 103
 Ken Rodgers
Nashinoki Shrine makes Lifestyle Changes .................................. 107
 Kirsty Kawano
Summer Rain .................................................................................... 111
 Lisa Twaronite Sone
Sudou Shrine .................................................................................... 119
 Malcolm Ledger
The Watcher ..................................................................................... 126
 Maria Danuco
"Keywords" of Kyoto ....................................................................... 129
 Mayumi Kawaharada
The Hills of Kyoto ............................................................................ 133
 Patrick Colgan
Kyotoyana ......................................................................................... 139
 Preston Keido Houser
Thinking Kyoto like a Mountain .................................................... 147
 Robert Weis
Kyoto Time ....................................................................................... 152
 Stephen Benfey
The Promise ...................................................................................... 154
 Tetiana Korchuk
Sound Travels ................................................................................... 157
 Tina deBellegarde
Kyoto's Nature *versus* My Apiphobia ............................................ 163
 Yuki Yamauchi

Appendix: Photographs ................................................................... A-1

# *A Word from the Editors*

It is with great pleasure that we offer this collection of literary works and photographs on the theme "The Nature of Kyoto." Our Anthology presents prose and poetry revealing many sides of this diverse and fascinating city. It caters to a number of reading styles, from those who like to dip in and out, discovering a new dimension of the ancient capital on each reading; to those who like to read from cover to cover in one sitting.

In selecting the theme of the Anthology, we wanted contributors to investigate the myriad aspects of Kyoto's "nature"—referring to both the natural world and the "inner nature" or soul of the city.

All authors either reside in Kyoto or have a special relationship with the city. Except for some competition winners, all are members of Writers in Kyoto (WiK). Our organization was established by John Dougill in 2015 to provide a sense of community and help foster a literary culture for English-language authors with Kyoto connections.

As our authors come from various countries, we followed the previous Anthology's policy of allowing each to use regional English spelling and punctuation rules, as long as they remained consistent within their individual pieces. We have italicized Japanese words, except for most proper nouns.

Not all of WiK's members contributed to this collection. If you would like to read a broader range of their works, our website (www.writersinkyoto.com) features new writing as well as historical pieces about Kyoto. It also provides a full listing of members and links to their writing, as well as details about how to join WiK and news about our upcoming events. In addition, WiK runs three Facebook groups, one closed (for members only) and two open to the public. We also hold numerous literary events in Kyoto, including book launches, poetry readings, workshops and dinner talks. If you are a writer with a connection to Kyoto, we encourage you to join WiK and make the most of these opportunities.

This Anthology also includes the top three winning pieces from the Sixth and Seventh Writers in Kyoto Competitions (2021 and 2022). As WiK's annual competition has evolved, we have devised ways in which to highlight a wider variety of global wordsmiths. WiK attained the generous support of Kyoto City for the prestigious Kyoto City Mayoral Prize in 2022. Instead of offering a Second Prize and Third Prize, we decided to showcase the top works of both a native English speaker (Yamabuki Prize) and non-native English speaker (Unohana Prize). Therefore, readers will note a difference in prize names within this particular Anthology. Congratulations again to all of the winners.

As Anthology editors, our sincere appreciation goes first and foremost to the authors who contributed their stories and photographs. Without their effort and imagination, and those of the competition winners, this book could never have taken shape. We would like to especially thank Rick Elizaga for his design work.

This Anthology is the fifth published by WiK. Jann Williams, WiK's Anthology Supervisor, provided invaluable and much-appreciated guidance, as did previous Anthology editors Rebecca Otowa and Karen Lee Tawarayama. Our gratitude also goes to Pico Iyer for writing our Anthology's Foreword. Finally, we would like to thank our families and friends for their love, support and understanding along the way, as we worked to create this Anthology.

*Kyoto, Tokyo and Luxembourg, Winter 2023*
Lisa Twaronite Sone & Robert Weis

FOREWORD
# The Rain upon the Rooftops
PICO IYER

The minute you step into Japan's thousand-year capital, it's hard not to start putting things into words. Yes, the train station where you arrived is a wild 22nd century labyrinth and the streets are dizzy with streaking lights and high-rise "pencil buildings." Nowhere is more madly in love with the latest and the fashionable. Yet everywhere, it's not difficult to see, are spirits alive in the hills, and around the sixteen hundred temples, as close to you as the winter chill on your neck.

Sitting in a Midtown office in New York City when very young, I heard a summons to Japan's ancestral home from Kenneth Rexroth and Gary Snyder, in part because both were so alert to all the ancient forces still governing the city of ladies and monks. Thomas Merton addressed the American poet Cid Corman as a monastic simply because he happened to live in Kyoto; Edith Shiffert, from Canada, spent half a century transcribing the seasons around her along the eastern hills as Ono no Komachi might have done a millennium before. By the time I touched down, in 1987, Diane Durston was excavating shops and traditions in hidden places that barely seemed to register the passing centuries.

What I didn't know enough about then were all the other visitors, from China and Germany and Ukraine, who were translating the city into their own tongues and contexts. Kyoto is one of those special places—like Venice, perhaps, or maybe St. Petersburg—that seem to belong to us all.

As I began making my way through the gifts presented in this collection, what struck me was how many of them are possessed by the old, even in the midst of zany fashions and crowded shopping arcades—old people, like the grandmother with difficult memories so hauntingly evoked by Lisa Twaronite Sone; old buildings, like the ones Rebecca Otowa fears will soon be razed to the ground; even those open-source cranes and crows that Ken Rodgers tunes in to, who might well have been cawing above Lady Murasaki while she was more or less inventing the novel. Always in Kyoto one is surrounded by presences much older and more durable than we are, which is what gives resonance to, say, Fernando Torres's bracing and often funny essay on all the ways Nature puts the Kyoto-ite in place (a bear in the lobby of the Westin Miyako Hotel!).

Poetry and meditation have always seemed the natural forms for the foreign writer in Kyoto; the visitor eager to advance some argument can feel like someone shouting in German in a hushed Parisian café. It's more elliptical and suggestive forms that seem most in tune with the sense of everything fading, even as that very sense of impermanence is part of the changeless music of the city.

Kyoto is the place for writing of all that is missing or vanished, a long wait through the night, as so beautifully suggested in Amanda Huggins' poem. It's the place where walking with a sweetheart along the Kamo River, or hearing John Dougill's wind through the bamboo groves, one instantly feels joined with generations of others who, whatever their language (or their silences), knew the same.

A newcomer to Kyoto is often greeted by Basho's celebrated lines: "Even in Kyoto / hearing the cuckoo's cry / I long for Kyoto." Yet regardless of how much is lost, or how different the place may be from the one you've created in your head, something at its heart remains, beneath—and sometimes because of—all the shifting surfaces. Every time I return to the pieces collected here, co-edited by a multi-phonic writer who recently brought Kyoto and its seasons to the National Museum of Luxembourg, I think of a poem that Basho didn't write: "Even far from Kyoto / reading of the cuckoo's cry / I hear the rain upon the rooftops."

Nara, November 2022

x

# Kyoto: Different Forms of Hypnosis

STEPHEN MANSFIELD

I am not a resident of Kyoto. I live along the ghost lines, the vaporous edges of Tokyo, perimeter suburbs that leave no trace of memory—the disfigured outer rings of the city, where you are more likely to find demolition crews, chain link fences, shuttered gaming halls, and used car dealerships than trees. Comparing the outskirts of Kyoto with my environs would be like confusing asphalt with foliage, a lush forest with a sewage outlet. And yet, in the midst of this map of degradation, I have tried to construct a green and pleasant land form, a folly as absurd as making a moss garden in the dead quarters of the Sahel.

In striking contrast, the roots and tubers of nature, moderated by the slow, hypnotic passage of time, reach deep into the urban fabric of Kyoto. Residents still have to contend with traffic, the inane blare of advertising, unsightly webs of power lines, and transgressive architectural implants, but they are mindful of nature countering, healing the blockages and hemorrhaging that generate anxiety disorders.

Zen holds that human energy and power are at their zenith when we attain a state of composed calm, one ideally induced by nature. This natural world mediates between the condition of separation and connection, inner and outer states of being, and Kyoto, predisposed to hosting the natural world, is that rarest of phenomena in Japan: a city where landscape and urbanscape merge. Applying geomantic principles to a physical structure, Kyoto's original grid system may have resembled something like a Chinese or Tibetan mandala of the kind found in esoteric or tantric Buddhism. By constructing a city with cosmic aspirations, the area itself could be understood as an object of veneration, a magnetic receiver for the powerful currents emanating from nature. In geomantic terms, such energy flows more beneficially when it passes along curved lines or undulations. In the formal geometry of Kyoto, the curve meets the right angle, rivers conform to the confinements of embankments, and the circulation of air is impeded by structural blocks. But nature, the great improviser, abhorrer of stagnation, discovers ways to build its own corridors and flows to reach the receptive mind, resulting in an effect akin to a trance state.

One of the effects of mild hypnosis of this kind, triggered in this instance by proximate nature, is the deceleration of time, the freeing of the mind from the grinding effects of motion and preoccupation. Something like a clinically therapeutic condition occurs when people spend time in contact with nature. Without the necessity of referencing the complex terminology of cognitive neuroscience, we sense instinctively the benefits of walking in a forest, an experience that lowers levels of the stress hormone cortisol, which affects blood pressure and the functioning of the immune system. In the same way, oblivious to research revealing that trees and plants emit aromatic compounds called phytoncides which produce biological changes similar to aromatherapy, we know instinctively that deep gulps of air in a natural setting enhance our sense of well-being. Similarly, it's hardly a revelation to learn that city residents are at higher risk of suffering from anxiety and mood disorders than their rural counterparts.

Where many of us wonder with vague awe at the pleasantly transformative spell cast by nature, psychiatrist and garden therapy advocate Sue Stuart-Smith has written in empirically tested detail about its restorative power. Beauty manifested in nature, she tells us, activates the emotional centers of the brain—in particular the medial orbital frontal cortex, which is associated with the release of endorphins, dopamine and creatinine, resulting in stress reduction. We learn that over-active, immune response-suppressing levels of salivary cortisol are lower in urban residents living within sight of verdant areas. Greenery, she continues, helps to activate the parasympathetic nervous system, offering relief from our task-oriented existence. An altogether superior alternative to antidepressants, supplements, and a whole pharmacopeia of available over-the-counter drugs, Kyoto offers the experience of immersive nature within a city, where rivers, plants, trees, and transplanted rocks act as convectors for the energies manifest in the mountains and forests that surround it.

Residents may not always be sensitized to the felicitous effects of the natural world that envelops them, or be aware of unconsciously experiencing hypnotic states of being, but they are its beneficiaries, in coming into frequent contact with its green and hilly perimeters and extraordinary endowment of gardens. In an interview with landscape designer Charles Chesshire, Kyoto-based garden scholar Gunter Nitschke noted that "even the most modern Japanese designer is less alienated from nature and its mysteries than a Western designer."

Nature has a persuasive hand in creating gardens, even as its purity is compromised by the reconceptions of design. In a sense, these man-made structures remain emissaries of nature, its duality, and the forces it embodies. Transfixed in time, but temporal, accommodators of both vitality and serenity, confined in space but boundless, gardens are organic artifacts, consciously conceived yet natural, the designer both interpreter and collaborator. Here, the flow of time is quite different from the coursing of work or social time. The deceleration that takes place produces a state of well-being that makes us calm but aware, relaxed but mindful, tranquil but alert. Akin to the Buddhist idea of true nature, there is an abiding conviction that, in the deepest recesses of mind and soul, there exists pure spirit, whose natural habitat is the garden. This can be sensed in the quieter landscapes at the edges of the city, where fecundity is a kind of opiate.

Leaving neurosis behind at the garden gate, I am often struck by the changes to my own state of being with extended exposure to these exquisite works of art. I reason that if beauty and a benevolent authority exist in these ancient gardens, a seamless unity capable of reconnecting us to an inherent order must also exist, given the accumulation of time, growth and erosion of matter, and residues of maturated wisdom. Our time within the stone and clay parameters of these mind sanctuaries may be constrained, but it is enough to re-energize us, clear out the static from our ears, reflect mindfully on the moment, and achieve equipoise.

Surrounded by dead or toxic planets, droning silence and magnum space, we are singularly fortunate to be inhabitants of a green and fertile world, even if that bounty is unevenly distributed. Gardens, the embodiment of that fecundity, empower us with the ability to do absolutely nothing, to still the restless mind, loosen stiff muscles, and counter life's obdurate headwinds. In a world ravaged as much by memory as the physical debris of war, destruction, overdevelopment and global sickness, gardens calm us, and even confront the debilitating fears and dread that seize us in the middle of the night. Unlike our own lives, Japanese gardens represent an ordered, collected and composed universe. They oblige us to acknowledge that we have strayed from an innate knowledge of the very world in which we live. Their richly encoded messages, the spells they cast on us, like powerful states of unconscious hypnosis that seek to stir up suppressed memories and experiences, tell us what we already know, but have lost touch with.

Kyoto may be the best of all possible places to experience the benign infiltrations of nature, to cultivate a sharper, more tempered intuition of the supercharged forces surging through air and earth.

※

**Stephen Mansfield** is a British writer and photographer. His work has appeared in over 60 magazines, newspapers and journals worldwide, including *The Geographical, The Middle East, Critical Asian Studies* and *Ikebana International*. He is a regular contributor to *The Japan Times, Kyoto Journal* and *Nikkei Asia*. He has had twenty books published. Japan-related titles include *Japanese Stone Gardens: Origins, Meaning, Form*; *Japan's Master Gardens: Lessons in Space & Environment*; and *Tokyo: A Biography*. He is currently writing a book for the publisher Thames & Hudson, on modern Japanese garden design.

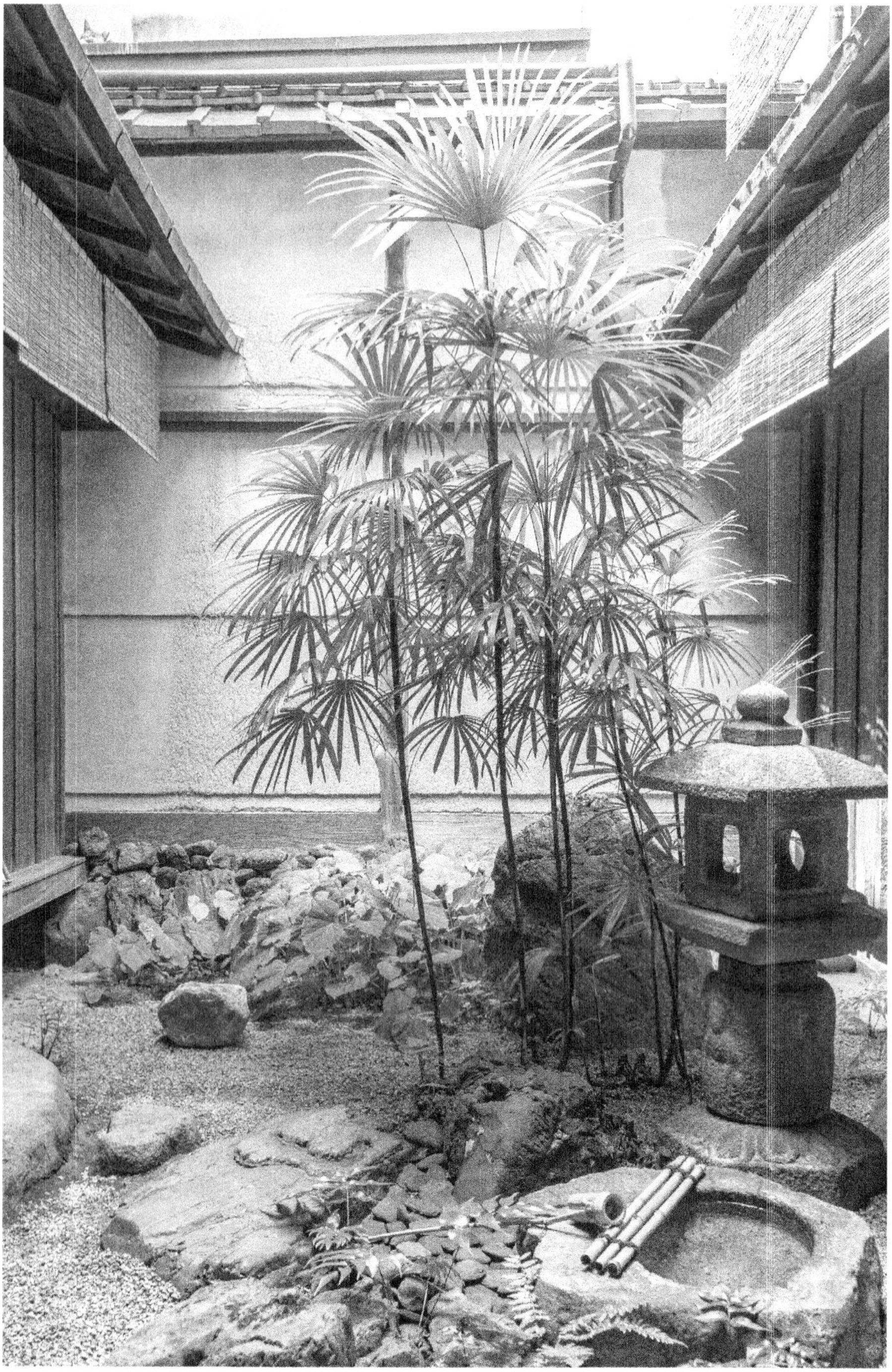

# The Pocket Garden

REBECCA OTOWA

*"Pocket garden" is my word for a small garden in the midst of a Kyoto* machiya *(town house).*
*This particular garden would be termed* nakaniwa *(inner garden).*

The winter sunshine, dim and warm, filtered down onto the trees in the pocket garden. It lay gently on the pine tree, one thin line to each needle. It touched the red berries and fans of small pointed red and green leaves of the heavenly bamboo, and the broader leaves of the smaller shrubs which draped themselves over the moss. It fell, rounded and fat, on each of the white river stones at the edge of the garden, and saved its most generous rays for the worn boards of the corridor where Ei-chan sat, gratefully warming his old bones and holding his hands out to the sunlight as to a fire.

This small two-story wooden house in the middle of Kyoto had been his home since he was born. How many years ago had that been? Ei-chan didn't know himself, but according to the health center records, he was now experiencing his ninety-fifth winter. He was a stooped, roly-poly old man, who favored knee-length fluffy vests on top of flannel shirts, and old-fashioned padded trousers. His body now was a compact shape, well suited to stooping and sitting cross-legged. He would have made a good *netsuke* figurine, if anyone had bothered to look at him long enough to carve him as an eight-centimeter ivory bead for holding a purse or tobacco pouch securely tucked into one's *kimono* sash. His face in the figurine would have resembled the god Ebisu, eternally smiling, plump and cheerful, ringed with whiskers.

Ei-chan (a child's nickname, by which he was still known around the neighborhood; his real name was Ei-ichiro) had been born here as the eldest son—his father was a craftsman in one of the neighborhood silk workshops. He had grown up in this small rabbit-warren of streets just wide enough for walking, had dashed around with friends narrowly avoiding the potted plants which crowded the doorways of the houses, and had stood in a line with the other children, sucking on brightly-colored sweets and staring big-eyed at the crowds of naked-limbed young men hefting the giant *mikoshi*, portable shrines carried through the larger streets nearby during local festivals. Later, Ei-chan himself had taken his turn at carrying the *mikoshi,* and around the same time, had followed his father into the silk workshop. He had also noticed the neighborhood sweetshop owner's well-grown daughter, marrying her with both families' approval and bringing her back to the house in the little lane.

They had been good years, as far as Ei-chan could remember, and they had all centered on the wooden house with the small space in the middle where the pocket garden grew. It was no bigger than the smallest of the rooms that surrounded it, but the red pine tree which was its best feature grew all the way up to the roof of the second story, its branches within reach of the railing around the open-air corridor deep under the eaves, with smaller trees and plants clustering around the base of its trunk. Ei-chan's mother had tended the small mossy space, which had looked the same all through the years. Later his wife had taken over, combing the moss, removing dead leaves, clipping stray branches of heavenly bamboo when they burgeoned upward from the root, deciding when the professional tree-trimmer would come, to sit all day atop his long ladder cutting off the excess pine needles with his little scissors.

Ei-chan knew how the garden looked in all seasons. There was a spindly plum which put forth small, dignified dark pink flowers, each on its own branch, in March. The heavenly bamboo showed a profusion of white flowers in summer, becoming cascades of red berries in winter. Some nameless bush had a few cute little buttons of light purple blossoms in autumn. Even the mosses on the ground had their changes—advancing and retreating, putting forth blossoms almost too small to see on the ends of minute green stalks. His favorite time was when light snow rested on the leaves, a different way on each leaf, and the river stones each wore its own round cap of white.

Since his wife had died the previous year, Ei-chan did his best to sweep up the heavenly bamboo leaves or the plum blossoms or the stray pine needles as they fell, but somehow it wasn't the same. Now Ei-chan lived in the house alone at the end of his long life, sitting on the wooden corridor, sometimes with a cup of tea, sometimes with a long-stemmed tobacco pipe, and gazing out at the pocket garden. His thoughts turned back to the sound of pounding children's feet and the smell of sun-warmed *futon*, all the signs of life that the old house had known throughout its long history.

Now he noticed that the sky was clouding over and the warmth of the winter sun had disappeared. He sat still as the large drifting clumps of snowflakes known as *botan-yuki* (peony snow) began to fall and lodge themselves amongst the foliage in the pocket garden. Ei-chan laughed with delight as a stray puff of wind planted one of the large snowflake clumps square on his nose. He felt as if he himself were a plant, a part of the pocket garden for a few moments.

"Ei-chan!" came a shrill cry, accompanied by the rattle of the front door sliding open—the next-door neighbor, Mrs. Tanaka. She was a youthful sixty years old, and had a vast and generous heart. Ei-chan, ignoring the entreaties of his children, refused to leave his house and still looked after himself, only accepting his evening meal from Mrs. Tanaka. She called again, "Are you there? Where are you?"

"Here," said Ei-chan, walking with his rocking gait down the corridor to the entranceway of the house. "What's going on?" Mrs. Tanaka didn't usually come at this time.

Seating herself on the *agari-to*, the wooden platform which divided the inner house from outside, she gazed out the still-open door. He sat next to her in his usual cross-legged posture. Together they watched the house opposite, only a couple of meters away, almost hidden behind the lacy curtain of falling snow.

"I just heard something that I thought you might like to know." She turned to gaze earnestly into his face. "The whole neighborhood is in an uproar! All the houses in the street behind us have been bought by a developer, who is going to put up a high-rise hotel! They expect that it will be finished by this time next year. There's to be a residents' meeting this weekend when they will explain the plan. Everyone on this street is also expected to attend."

Ei-chan swiftly calculated the direction of the new construction relative to their houses. It was toward the west. A large building there would mean no sunlight in the afternoon and evening. The house would be colder from autumn through to spring. And—even more important—the pocket garden would get next to no sun at all during the day. Perhaps a little just at noon, that was all. And instead of a nice blue sky, or clouds, or pink of sunset, there would be an uncompromising wall of windows, many of which would look directly into his house.

He put his head in his hands.

Mrs. Tanaka remarked, "There will be a lot of changes. It will be noisier, that's for sure, all those cars coming and going, to say nothing of the noise of the construction itself. Maybe dusty, too. I wonder where all the people living in those houses will go. What about Mr. Ishida—he's bedridden. And the Matsumotos—where will they end up?" She continued to muse aloud, aware of Ei-chan's distress, but in the Japanese way, she tried to make this disaster into something felt by an entire group of people, with individual problems subsumed into it. "Well," she said briskly, standing up, "I'll bring your dinner at six as usual. You like fish? How about some nice yellowtail tonight? Braised with soy sauce and sugar?"

She left, closing the door, and Ei-chan stood up slowly and went back to his seat looking out on the pocket garden. Each leaf and pine needle held up its little burden of snow. These plants had no idea of what was in store for them. Things were changing all over the city. Now it was the turn of the houses behind them, but at some point, it would be the turn of Ei-chan and Mrs. Tanaka and all their neighbors. The pocket garden would be uprooted and carried away by a developer's power shovel. The years of work and awareness and joy would be over.

These wooden houses had stood here a mere two hundred years in the long history of Kyoto. Some older edifices, barely imaginable, which stood here before had been swept away. The people who had been living here then weren't carried as individuals in anyone's memory. Ei-chan and Mrs. Tanaka wouldn't be either. They would become part of the vast river of humanity that had counted this particular area of land, cupped by the mountains, their home. The plants, the dignified old pine, the plum and heavenly bamboo with their brave flowers, were part of the same river of life as well. All would have to give up their places to whatever came later. That was the way of things.

Ei-chan ate and enjoyed his dinner of braised fish that night. Afterwards, when Mrs. Tanaka had taken away the dishes, he returned to his seat on the wooden corridor and gazed out at the pocket garden. The full moon was up now, and half of the garden was lit by a crazy bluish-white luminosity, the other half in deep shadow where the line of the roof fell. Ei-chan sat there for a long time, as the line moved across the garden. Eventually it was all in shadow, the glimmer of snow alone showing where the plants, stones, and moss were.

Mrs. Tanaka couldn't say why, but she went the next morning and opened Ei-chan's sliding front door with its usual rattle. There was no answer to her cheery call. She slipped off her shoes and stepped up onto the *agari-to*, walking cautiously and calling at intervals, venturing far into the house where she had never been before.

She noticed the open glass door opening onto the corridor next to the pocket garden. Cold air was wafting into the house. As she moved to close it, she noticed a dark shape on the surface of the white snow just under the pine tree, half-hidden by the plum and heavenly bamboo branches. She didn't want to step down into the garden in stocking feet, so she strained to see from where she stood.

It was Ei-chan. Sometime during the night he had crawled into his pocket garden, to be among the plants he loved.

Mrs. Tanaka nodded once, in a kind of accolade, before leaving the house and going to raise the alarm.

※

**Rebecca Otowa** has been living in Japan continuously since 1978, and in Kyoto 1978 to 1984. In 1981 she married the 19th-generation heir to a large farmhouse in Shiga prefecture. She has lived there, raising two sons, being mama to 7 cats, and pursuing her great loves, drawing and writing, for 36 years. She has published three books with Tuttle: *At Home in Japan* (2010), *My Awesome Japan Adventure* (2013), and *The Mad Kyoto Shoe Swapper and other stories* (2019), all self-illustrated.

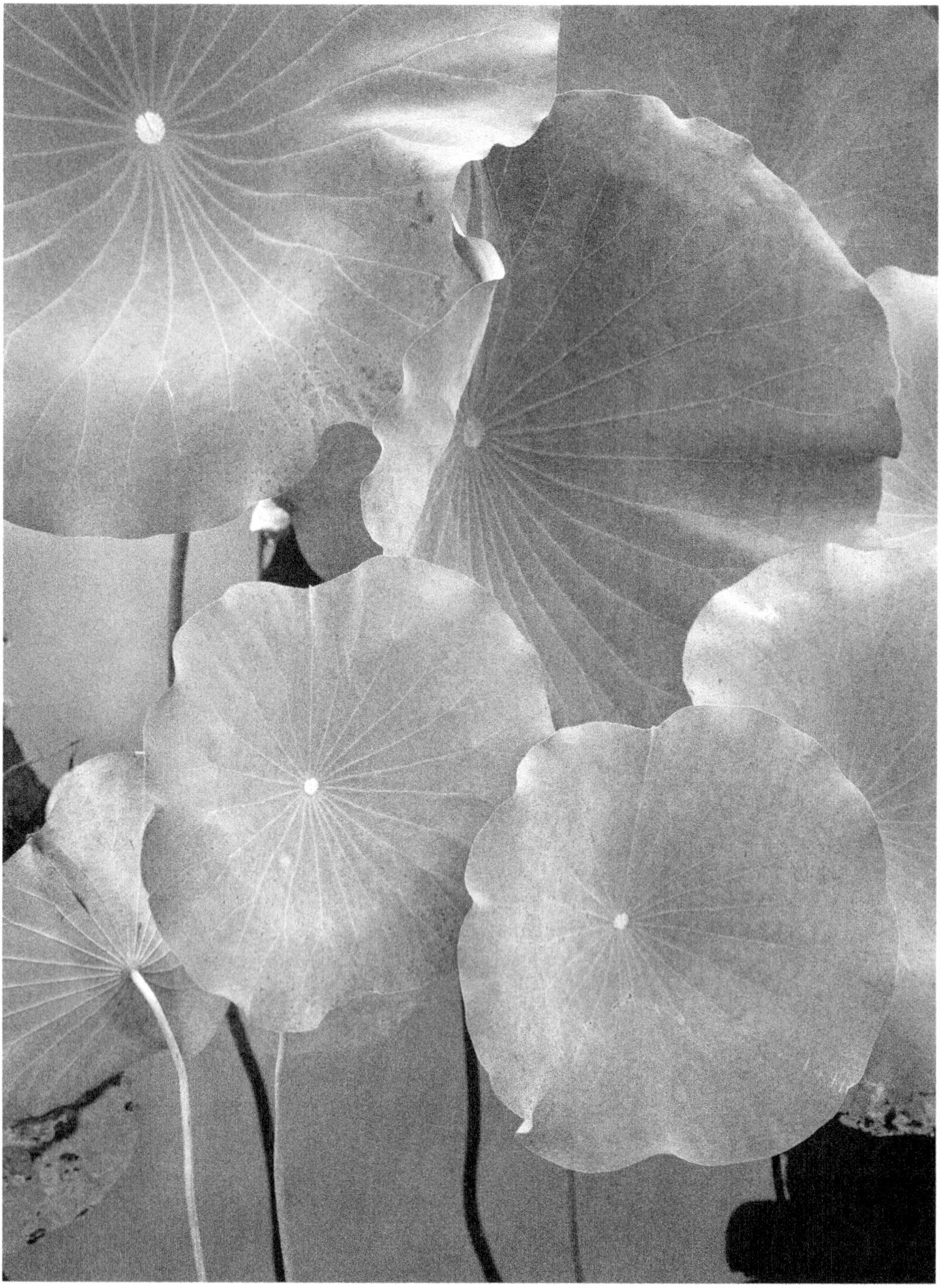

# Lotus 蓮

JOHN EINARSEN

The lotus has been admired and cultivated from India to East Asia for thousands of years. Tightly curled leaves ascend and unfurl from muddy ponds, then buds, culminating in large yet delicate blossoms that are pure, radiant, and otherworldly. It is easy to see why this flower, reaching towards the sky, has become a metaphor for spiritual growth and enlightenment, and why lotus iconography graces every Buddhist temple in Kyoto. Lotus are often grown in *hanchi*, the small rectangular ponds with low-arched bridges that originally demarcated the sacred space of a Zen temple. Such ponds can be found at Nanzen-ji, Tenryu-ji, Kennin-ji, To-ji and Tofuku-ji. Unfortunately, all of them are fenced off except the tiny one at Nanzen-ji, which is sandwiched between a parking lot for tour buses and the official temple lodgings.

What a delight it was for me to discover lotus when I first came to Japan. They have been a steadfast companion for many years. For a visual artist, the lotus offers a stunning diversity of bold, elegant forms that transform fantastically over the course of a year. A visit to the lotus pond always brings a gift of something strange and beautiful, and a reminder that nature is an unsurpassed, and always surprising, creator of beauty that touches the human heart.

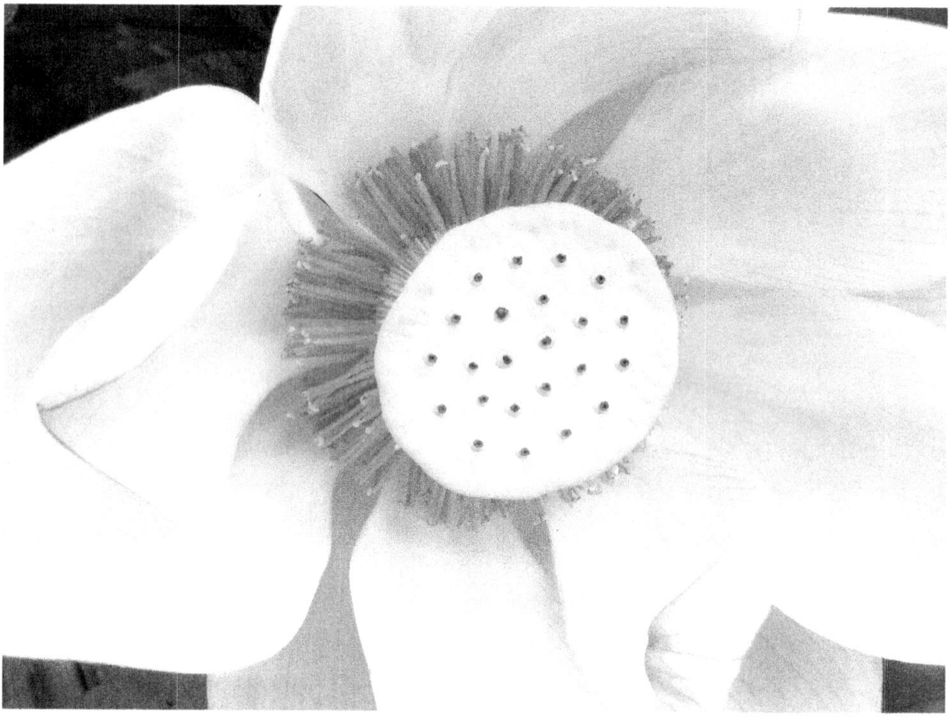

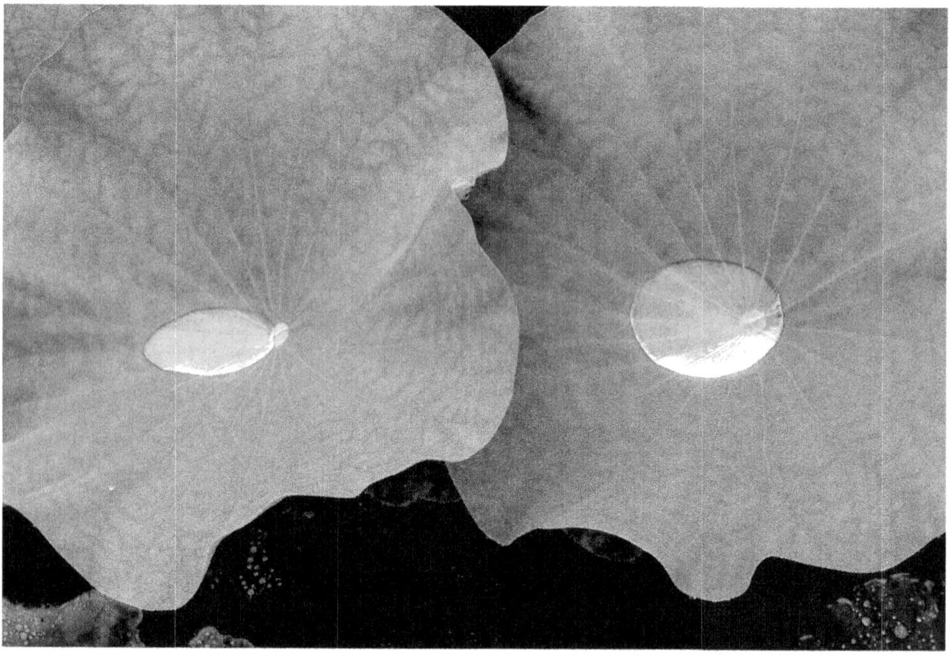

✺

**John Einarsen**'s books include *Kyoto: The Forest Within the Gate* (with poet Edith Shiffert, and others), *Small Buildings of Kyoto*, Vol. I & II, *Zen Gardens and Temples of Kyoto* (with John Dougill) and *Curtain Motif*. His new book, *This Very Moment*, was published last fall and is a collection of his Miksang photographs. He is also the founding editor of *Kyoto Journal* which he began with other poets and writers in 1986. From 2013–2015 he served as an advisor to *The Japan Times* and in 2013 received the Commissioner's Award of the Japanese Cultural Affairs Agency.

WRITERS IN KYOTO COMPETITION | 2021 **SECOND PRIZE**

# Love on a Low Flame

AMANDA HUGGINS

The house feels hollow now you've gone
and there's no one to call out to
when the DJ plays our favourite song.

I long for the familiar sound of your key in the lock,
your voice in the hallway
at the same time each day.

*Tadaima!*

I listen for your footsteps in the street below,
hear the tinkle of laughter, sweet as temple bells,
as girls hurry by, kimonos bright with peonies.

When summer wanes, the breeze spins restless leaves,
tangles wind chimes, rattles paper screens,
watches lanterns dance in empty doorways.

Sparrows take their roll call on the wire
and a lone heron flies low along the Kamo
with all Kyoto's quiet beauty stowed beneath his wings.

So now I will wait out winter, warm our love on a low flame,
fashion its wings from fallen feathers,
anchor it with stones.

I whisper to you in the dark,
breathe my greeting into cupped hands,
hold it close to my ribs in readiness for your return.

*Okaeri!*

※

**Amanda Huggins** is the author of the novellas *All Our Squandered Beauty* and *Crossing the Lines*, as well as four collections of stories and poetry. She has received numerous awards for her travel writing and short fiction, and her debut poetry collection, *The Collective Nouns for Birds*, won a Saboteur Award in 2020.

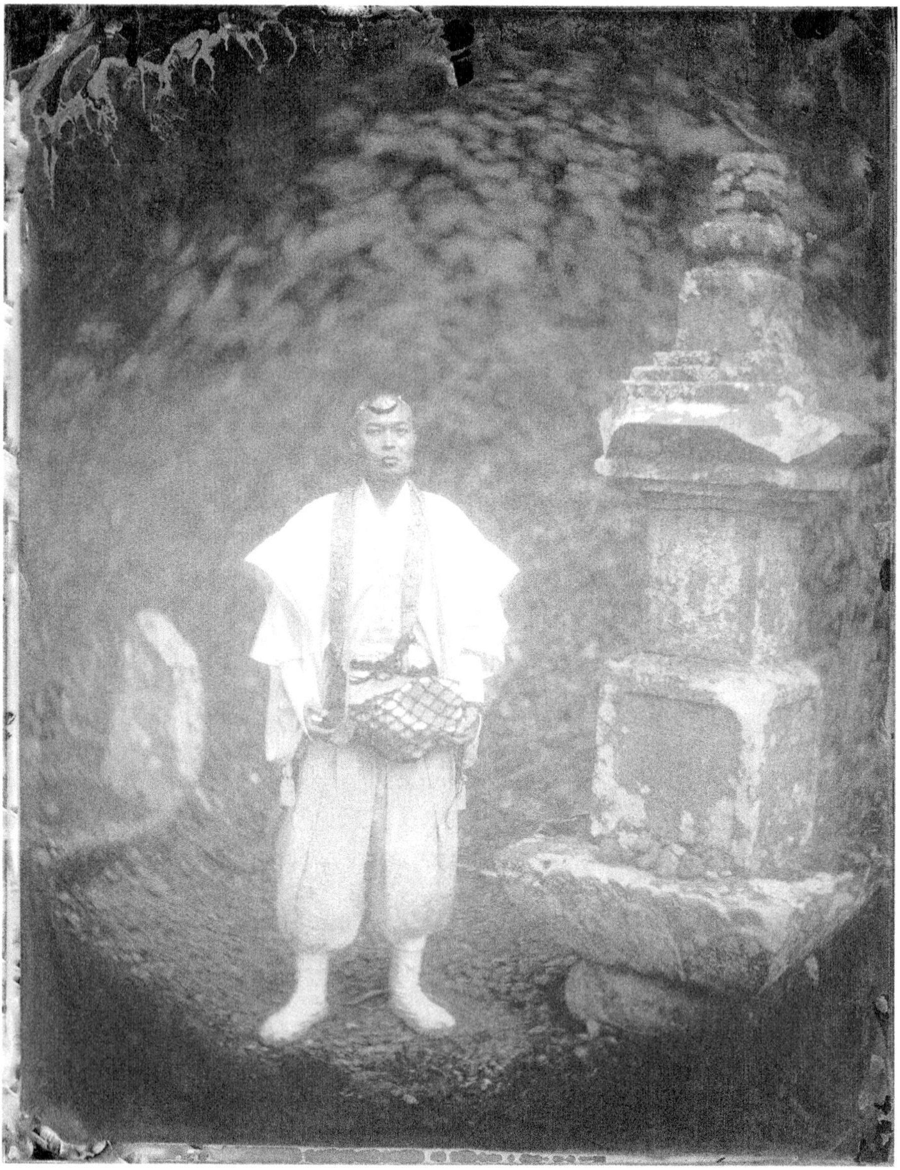

# The Graveyard of Homyo-in

EVERETT KENNEDY BROWN

The path from Mii-dera to Homyo-in was cool and soothing beneath my bare feet. I'd walked this way before, so I wasn't concerned about any sharp roots or rocks. In fact, the path was pounded flat by the feet of monks who'd made their way up here over the centuries. I could feel their vestiges in the shadows.

At the top of the hill I reached the gate to Homyo-in temple and walked into the outer garden. I could see the lights of fishing boats twinkling down on Lake Biwa, and towering against the pre-dawn sky was Mt. Mikami, silhouetted like a sacred pyramid.

Every time I came here, I felt something special. I felt it the first time I entered this garden soon after moving to Kyoto. There was an inner clarity here that I had rarely experienced in my previous life.

I walked over to the contoured rocks that overlooked the pond. They had been placed here a long time ago, but I wasn't sure when. I found them ideal for sitting. I'd come before dawn and gaze at the pond as the color of the water changed from shades of grey to pastel orange.

A blue fog hung over the pond this morning. It would have made a beautiful photograph, I thought; but I had no desire to carry a camera. I wanted my hands and eyes to be free, so that I could retrieve a sense of weightlessness that I had lost during my years of working as a photojournalist.

I never photographed wars, nor experienced any real danger; except for those trips to Fukushima, or that night at a sumo wrestler party when one of Putin's cronies showed up and I was forced to leave.

What was killing me wasn't the danger, but the daily grind and the adrenaline I felt every time the dark angels of power and celebrity passed in front of my lens. I felt as if my soul was being sucked away.

Now I no longer lived in other people's shadows. After moving to Kyoto, I could finally stand on the ground and feel the coolness of the earth beneath my feet. I was ready now to tell my own story.

I met the temple priest on a previous visit. He was an older man and quite energetic. He seemed curious about why I came to this remote temple and invited me in for tea.

We spent the whole afternoon talking about art and Esoteric Buddhism and discovered we had a similar passion for the past. He told me that I was not the first American with these interests to visit the temple.

It was quite a long time ago, the priest said—the late 19$^{th}$ century to be exact. There were two gentlemen from Boston who came to see the temple scrolls and bronze buddhas. After several visits the men became intimate with the priest at that time. Up on the hill I could find the two men's graves, the priest told me.

I could almost see those two Boston gentlemen here in the garden. Their memories seemed to linger around the contoured rocks where they would sit in their stiff suits watching as the moon rose over lake Biwa. They'd spend hours here talking of art and life, and occasionally they would pause, and with nicely manicured fingers one of them would flick ashes from their cigarette into the pond.

Those two Americans lived in a different time. It was an age when the aura of dead poets was still palpable to the skin. I'm referring to the poets that the priest talked about who used to walk across the hills from Kyoto for moon-viewing parties here in the garden.

So much has changed since then. The contoured rocks remain, but the noise of the city invades the garden's silence. First there were cars and then radios and TVs. Now there are computers that program our nerves in ways that distract the soul from living an open life.

Is it the fate of modern man to stare up at the moon, lost in private thoughts of space travel? It was different for those poets who sat by the pond, chatting, drinking sake, and writing poetry about moonlight, as it rippled across the surface of the pond.

I was ready now to go to the edge of the garden and find the path up to the graves. As I approached the forested path I stopped for a moment to adjust my eyes to the darkness. I could feel something watching me.

It was neither a human, nor an animal; but was perhaps one of those lingering spirits that Kyoto people talk about—the ones that wander in these eastern hills. But I wasn't here to see ghosts, I was simply following the urge that brought me here.

After waking up in the middle of the night, I had found it impossible to go back to sleep. So I put on some clothes, and feeling a need to walk, I ended up here at the temple.

For some reason I didn't feel any fear walking up the path. Even in my bare feet I felt a sense of inner calm, as if I were being guided by some magnetic force.

When I got to the top of the hill I came to five large rocks. They were stacked on top of each other to form a Buddhist pagoda. On each stone was a Sanskrit letter that represented one of the five elements of nature. They reminded me that some part of us returns to a kind of cosmic pool of energy when our bodies die.

This was the first grave, the place where Ernest Fenollosa was buried. After the renowned art historian's death in London, his ashes were sent here by his wife. She knew this was his favorite place in Japan.

I had always felt an odd kinship with Fenollosa. Since my student days, I had read all his books and was inspired by his life in Japan. I was surprised when the priest told me about Fenollosa's connection with Homyo-in temple. The story had an unusual resemblance to my own.

I was leaving an unhappy marriage of twenty years when I arrived in Kyoto. One could say it was a typical mid-life crisis story. I needed to retrieve something missing in my life and had started a relationship with a younger woman with whom I was passionately in love. What makes the story different was that we ended up in a little Buddhist temple in the eastern hills of Kyoto where we could build our new life together.

When Fenollosa left his unhappy marriage, he quickly remarried his young assistant at the Museum of Fine Arts. All of that was a bit too much for Boston society and the scandal forced Fenollosa out of his good job at the museum.

The newlyweds found their life in Boston untenable, so they packed their bags and sailed for Japan. When they arrived at Homyo-in the priest promptly arranged living quarters for them in the back of the temple.

During the years that Fenollosa lived in Japan before, he and the priest had become close friends. He often visited the priest with his mutual friends, Okakura Tenshin (the art expert and author of *The Book of Tea*) and William Bigelow (a prominent art collector and patron). The four of them often spent many evenings together talking about art and life.

I was surprised to learn that their intimacy went much deeper. The three art experts were like soul brothers, the priest informed me.

They had even been ordained as Esoteric Buddhist priests at the temple.

When I heard this, I suddenly thought about a photograph I had found in a used bookstore off Harvard Square nearly forty years ago. I was thumbing through a book about 19th century travelers in Japan when I came to a page with a photograph of someone who was clearly not a typical tourist.

It was a photo of a handsome and robust man, but what caught my attention were the straw sandals on his feet and the pilgrim's staff in his right hand. He was dressed as a Japanese mountain pilgrim.

I was curious about who this man was, so I bought the book to find out. I discovered that it was Bigelow, the other American who was buried right next to Fenollosa.

When the priest told me that they had been ordained as esoteric priests, I had a sudden intuition. Perhaps that photo of Bigelow had been taken in the garden?

Other questions started flooding my mind, such as why those three leading art experts become esoteric priests? Were they seeking some kind of spiritual insight into Japanese art that simple scholarship couldn't provide them?

This got me thinking. The temple complex of Miidera had been a major center for Shugendo, a tradition of mountain esoteric asceticism for over a thousand years. Its priests were renowned for their arduous training, such as walking long distances in the mountains and praying in cold waterfalls near the temple.

I had become interested in Shugendo after leaving my photojournalism career as a way to understand Japanese people's spiritual relationship with nature. I'd met a Shugendo priest who even introduced me to what he called the Naka-ima.

He described it as a mystical state, a kind of parallel reality similar to the Aboriginal Dreamtime, where one could "see" into the past and future.

I wondered if Fenollosa and Bigelow had encountered the Naka-ima in their esoteric training? The priest at Homyo-in certainly must have been familiar with such things. I looked for clues in both Fenollosa and Bigelow's writings, but couldn't find any answers.

Such esoteric things were usually kept secret in 19th century Japan. But even so, a few of the more unconventional Western travelers, such as the astronomer William Lowell and the mystic, Madame Blavatsky, wrote in detail about this little known spiritual world.

In my travels around Japan I had encountered vestiges of this world. I had even photographed the male *shamen* on Mt. Ontake and Noro women in Okinawa. I felt it was important to record these ancient traditions while they still remained. To do this I started working with hand-made glass negatives and made fine art prints that I exhibited and sold to promote this cause.

Standing there in the darkness in front of Fenollosa's grave, I closed my eyes. I then arched my back the way a cat does after a long nap and took a deep breath. I then bowed my head to better feel the silence.

After some time I began to feel a cool breeze coming from the silence beyond the grave. I turned my attention towards the coolness and began to feel the fog of my past slowly clear away.

Over the years I'd often seen myself as like a stray cat with nine lives. How many times had I found myself in some dark alley not living the life I was born to? I'd done a lot of things and suffered my share of setbacks, but all of that was behind me now. All those misadventures were simply part of learning how to live an open life.

As I stood there in the darkness I began to feel the lightness I had been seeking. My sense of time was expanding. The weight of more than one hundred years that separated me from Fenollosa, that distance was slipping away. I was able to gaze into the hallway of time and see my own historical moment.

The breeze was shifting. It would be dawn soon. I was ready now to go down the hill and join the chatter with those dead poets.

※

**Everett Kennedy Brown** is a photographer, writer and founder of the Kyoto Kaisho Foundation. He is using an 8x10 camera and hand-made glass negatives to create a series of books and limited-edition prints that illustrate Japan's deep culture. His innovative imagery have been featured on CNN, NHK, and TED talks and are in the permanent collections of museums in Japan, Europe and the United States. In 2013 he was awarded the Japanese Government's Cultural Affairs Agency Commissioner's Award in recognition of his creative activities.

**WRITERS IN KYOTO COMPETITION** | **2022 YAMABUKI PRIZE**

# Sudden Tsukimi

C. GREENSTREET

We stopped for *tsukimi* by the darkened delta of the Kamogawa. None of us intended to pause our post-work slog from the station, but it was too glorious to ignore. Our silhouettes arranged on the bridge, all strangers, to witness its arrival over the mountain shadows in the east.

Hushed voices as we bathed in the moonlight, rich and yellow like the yolk of a good egg. The murmuring river carried on below our feet, glimmering like our faces, now alive.

Elsewhere we would not see each other so. On the train, in line at the Fresco, waiting dutifully at the crosswalk of an empty street. No full golden moonlight, and here too it soon passed.

Our shadows scattered, dragging along pieces of that light. In our phones, in our poems, in our thoughts as we softly slid back *izakaya* doors. We'd needed the moon to lift our gazes, a brief celestial reminder to be human.

※

**C. Greenstreet** is an American archivist whose fascination with historical curiosities began in Kyoto, where he spent several years living, learning, and exploring. When not organizing old things, he writes as much as he can and edits the burgeoning whimsical horror magazine, *Kyoto Cryptids*.

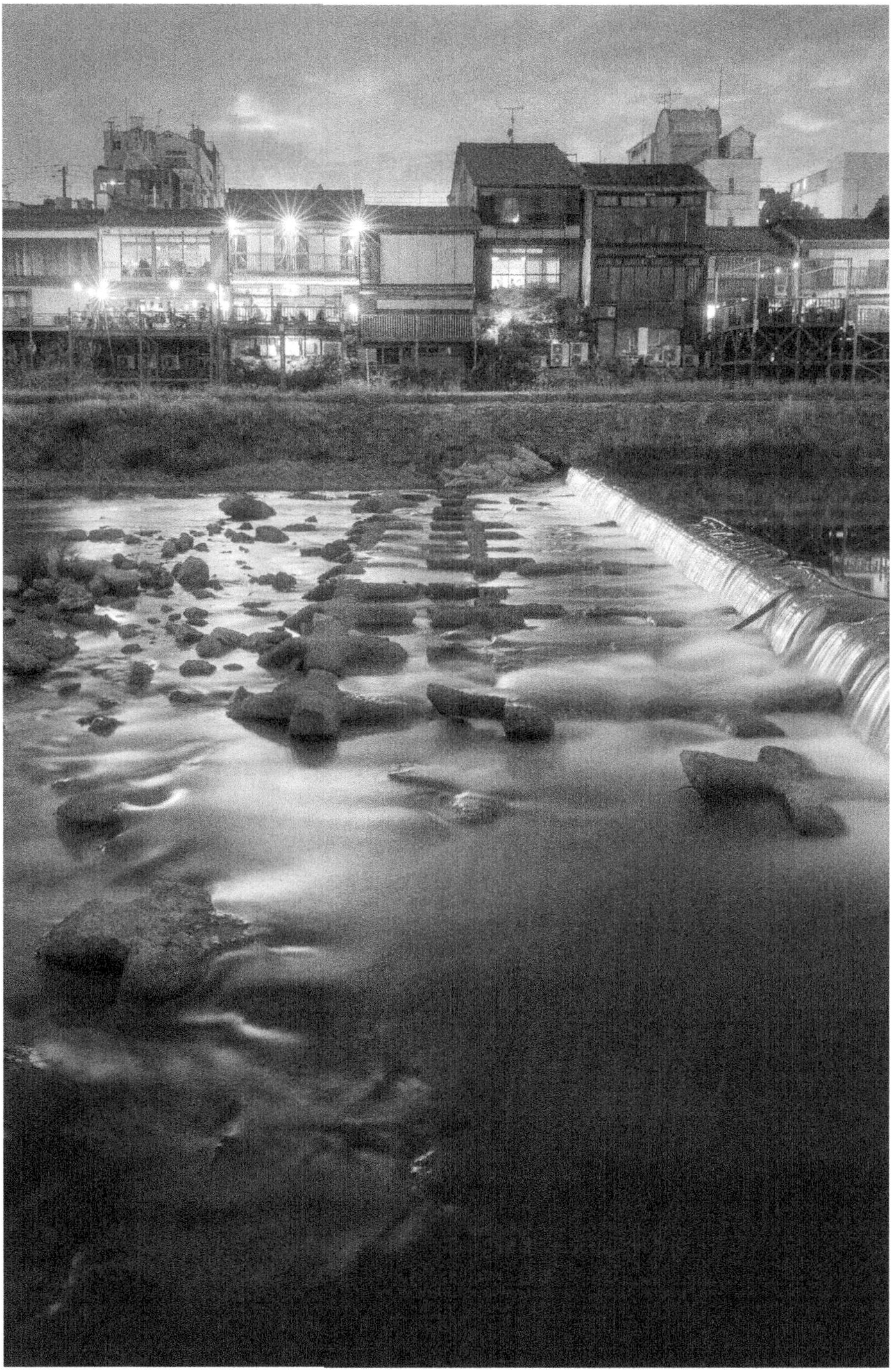

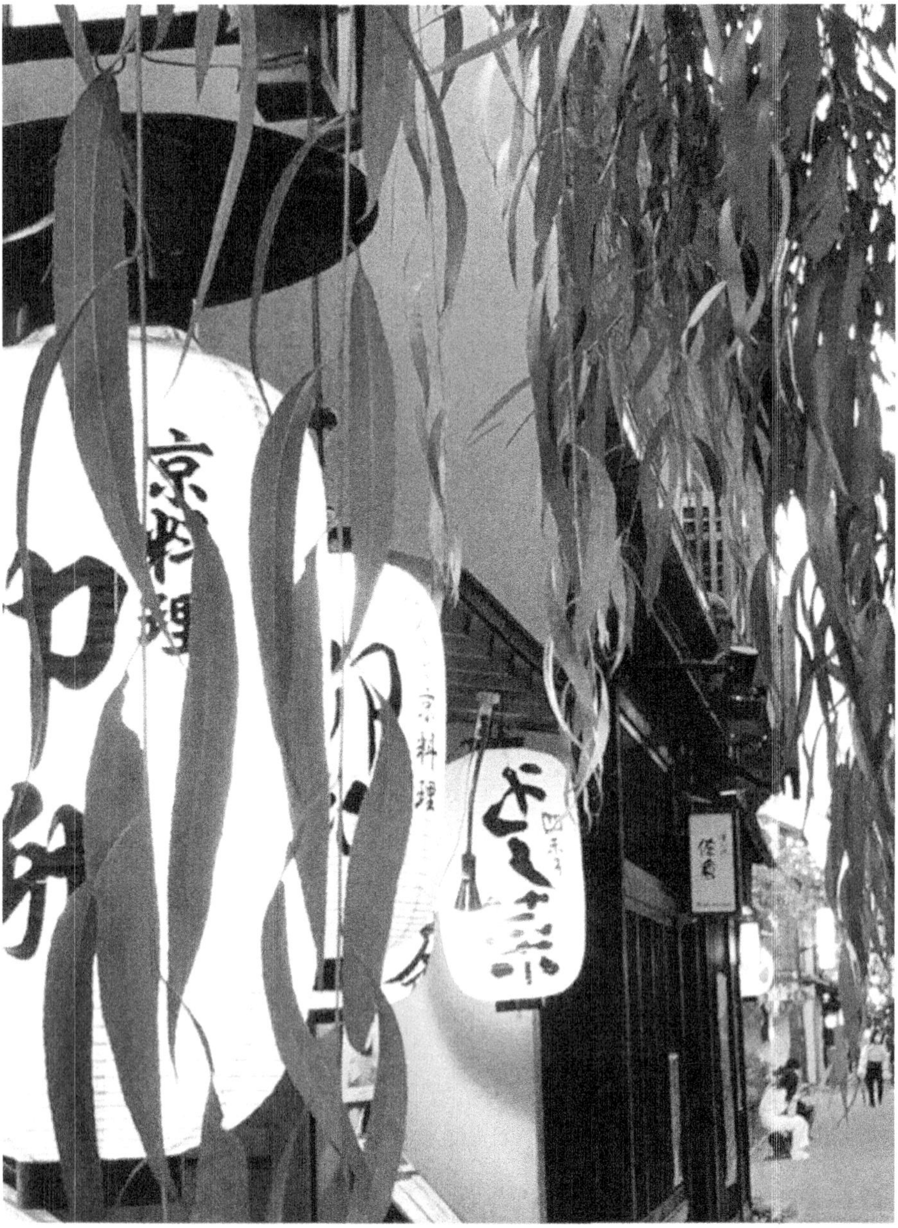
京料理

# For Love of the Octopus God

ELAINE LIES

Evening. It may be hot and thick, with the sun just barely starting to dip in a sullen red ball down towards the mountains in the west; or it's biting, breath rising in clouds from the mouths of the people, in groups of two or three, sauntering down the street below the willows. Or it's full dark, and my legs ache from walking the river, down past the trees with their gray herons settling in for sleep.

The walk there is like foreplay, every time. I may drift down Pontocho, its wooden house fronts blank faces hiding secrets, so many with signs seeking renters these days. I stare down narrow alleys where red lanterns have begun to glow, pass the park where buskers—both hopeful and hopeless—occasionally strum guitars. Smells tease out: the dark, sweet-sour beckoning of *okonomiyaki*, the sizzle of *yakitori*. The pillowy caress of rice in steamy glory.

I am not tempted. But my stomach growls. It is time.

I cut across to Kiyamachi, turn left. It always seems farther away than it is, and if I've been away for a while I start worrying: is it still there? So many restaurants fail every year, after all. Since I started coming, there have been three major earthquakes, countless typhoons, economic rises, economic falls. A pandemic. The street has seen an influx of grease and sleaze, maid cafes and *shisha* bars, chain drinkeries. The abandoned school and its darkened yard that for so long was my landmark, its blackness in the heart of playland both soothing and a little spooky, has been turned into a hotel so expensive I could never stay there.

I miss the darkness of the past. It clings, a scrim of memory layered over the bright new building with its soft green yard, the mille-feuille that is my Kyoto after so many years.

But I am here, and I am hungry. I look for the white wall, the red sign; I rattle open the heavy door. I enter the Temple of the Octopus God.

The *mama-san*'s automatic *Irasshaimase* turns into an *ohhhh* and then *Okaerinasai!* The man in the red rugby shirt, who I thought for decades was her son, nods; unasked, he draws me a beer and grins as he sets it on the counter in front of me, where that day's wonders lie heaped in bowls along the counter—bowls that, I've learned, the *mama-san* had made herself during a pottery phase.

I drink deeply. I sigh.

I am home.

\*\*\*\*\*\*\*\*\*\*\*

*Entering the Octopus Road.*

That's what I thought its name was for years, from that first Friday night now nearly four decades ago.

I was living in a *gaijin* house with the toilet far out back, past an open courtyard into which snow drifted down on hushed nights as I walked shivering out below the 2:00 a.m. skies. I made huge pots of *oden* that I ate for a week, or fried cabbage and onions with eggs. At night I pored over Japanese newspaper editorials about "nuclear arms reduction" and "the Cold War," looking up almost every *kanji* in my battered Nelson's dictionary. Copying the new ones over at least 25 times, to learn them, hunched over a table on the *tatami* in my down jacket to keep warm.

One Friday, friends dragged me to a free movie—maybe Ozu, maybe Oshima?—at the Japan Society downtown. I dressed up—wore a sweater, put in my contacts, draped on earrings. And after the movie they took me out. We entered the Octopus Road.

A narrow counter took up most of the tiny place, which I remember as dark and shadowy, down a labyrinthine alley. My first beer for weeks, then maybe a *chuhai*. Strange, wonderful food—tiny whole octopuses simmered in an *umami*-rich broth, chunks of *kabocha* that melted, sweet and mealy, on my tongue. And hot, pillowy, eggy balls of wonder studded inside with octopus, an elegant *takoyaki* cousin.

Along the counter were bowls of other riches I vowed to get back and try.

A contact irritated my eye, so I cried and cried, just one eye, all night, furtive in the corner with my tissues, as the *mama-san* and an older woman made soft sounds of distress, plying me with hot sake. But my tongue remembered and loved the food.

I was a convert.

In many ways, I have never left.

\*\*\*\*\*\*\*\*\*\*

Its name is "The Octopus God," I now know; or maybe even "monster"—a water creature that hangs out with the Eel Princess when she's not deep into the ocean, weaving on her loom. But the eight-legged creature outside is cute, dressed for fun with a *hachimaki* around its head, eyes bright.

Each night proceeds with stately pace. At least at first.

I look up at the man, I smile. We might say a little—how long I am here, when did I come—but he's too busy for a lot of chit-chat. So I order.

*Akashi-yaki.*

He clicks on the gas burner, sets down the cast-iron pan, dips batter from a huge plastic bucket into each of the eight round molds. As these firm up, he studs them with a chunk of octopus, then deftly turns them one after the other with a skewer. A tiny bowl of soup in which shreds of *benishoga* float is set before me; I breathe in its sea-smelling steam. Then the pan is upended on a worn red platter which is set down before me, with just the hint of a flourish.

*Akashi-yaki* are like clouds. Each soft, eggy morsel nearly melts on my tongue around the chunk of octopus, a bit chewy, that tastes of the ocean and of waves. I close my eyes. My hands pause in the air, chopsticks unmoving.

Life is, in that moment, still and perfect.

To keep from gobbling them down in undue haste, I choose other dishes and take delicious alternating bites: rich stewed beef tendon, melting mellow fat perfectly complemented by a morsel of golden *karashi; kabocha;* slivered *renkon,* simmered salty-sweet with ground beef. In the winter, there's *oden*: steaming boiled egg, a round of *daikon* that resists my teeth for a second before melting in all its salty, savory glory, and tiny stuffed cabbages whose juicy filling runs down my chin. Crispy fried *yuba* dipped in salt.

Each night, at some moment, the *mama-san* goes around the three-sided counter in this bigger space to which they moved years ago, holding out presents: crisp wafer sandwiches filled with orange creme, slices of perfectly-ripe persimmon on a tiny plate, bean-paste *manju* from somewhere in northern Japan. She tells the room who is the giver, and they'll lift a glass to us as we all thank them.

I have recognized regulars. Sometimes, they have recognized me.

I have been invited to *karaoke* by another customer. As we leave the *karaoke* bar at midnight, the opening elevator door reveals a *geisha*, in all her elegance, less than an arm's length away.

I have debated the merits of *Jane Eyre* with PhD students, in Japanese, and I've discussed how much Kyoto has changed with a woman in her sixties who has never moved from her neighborhood by Nijo Castle.

The *chuhai* are poured with a generous hand.

Once or twice I have gotten very drunk, and drifted out into a Kiyamachi where the willows danced below the white lights and the stars, very glad my hotel was so close. Or I walked past the still Pontocho Kaburenjo down towards the river and saw a gray heron in the water, staring wistfully at the lights and the laughter—lonely, with a distance I too have known.

But not here.

I was here in November 2020, a break between the waves of pandemic States of Emergency that shut everything down, taking a break from my solitary days working alone in my house in Kanto.

There was no vaccine yet.

We tried keeping our masks on between bites, but soon it was hot inside, voices rose, and we were all trying to open gingko nuts a customer had brought, boasting about our techniques. One man down the counter tried his teeth, another *hashi*. The woman next to me smashed madly with the bottom of her beer *joki* as I tried hitting them with my fist. We laughed and laughed and laughed. And I realized: how much I had missed all this.

I felt human again, for that day. Alive.

I have since learned there's another meaning to its name, one that could refer to priests with their bald heads, their efforts to bring enlightenment. "Octopus Leading to Nirvana."

*In this* izakaya, *I'm already there.*
*This is my practice. Here do I pray.*

***************

The *mama-san* is growing old. Her hair has grayed and gone black again. She is losing weight.

The man-who-is-not-her-son is 62. His white hair is thinner now. His rugby shirts faded.

There will come an end someday that is unfathomable.

But until then I will eat *Akashi-yaki*, every time I am in Kyoto. I will drink beer.

I will laugh. I will live.

※

**Elaine Lies** has lived in Japan for more than half her life, in Yokohama, Kyoto (twice), Iwate and Tokyo. Despite being an impoverished student at the time, her months in Kyoto during her second visit were some of the best of her life. Her favorite *izakaya* in Japan is also there.

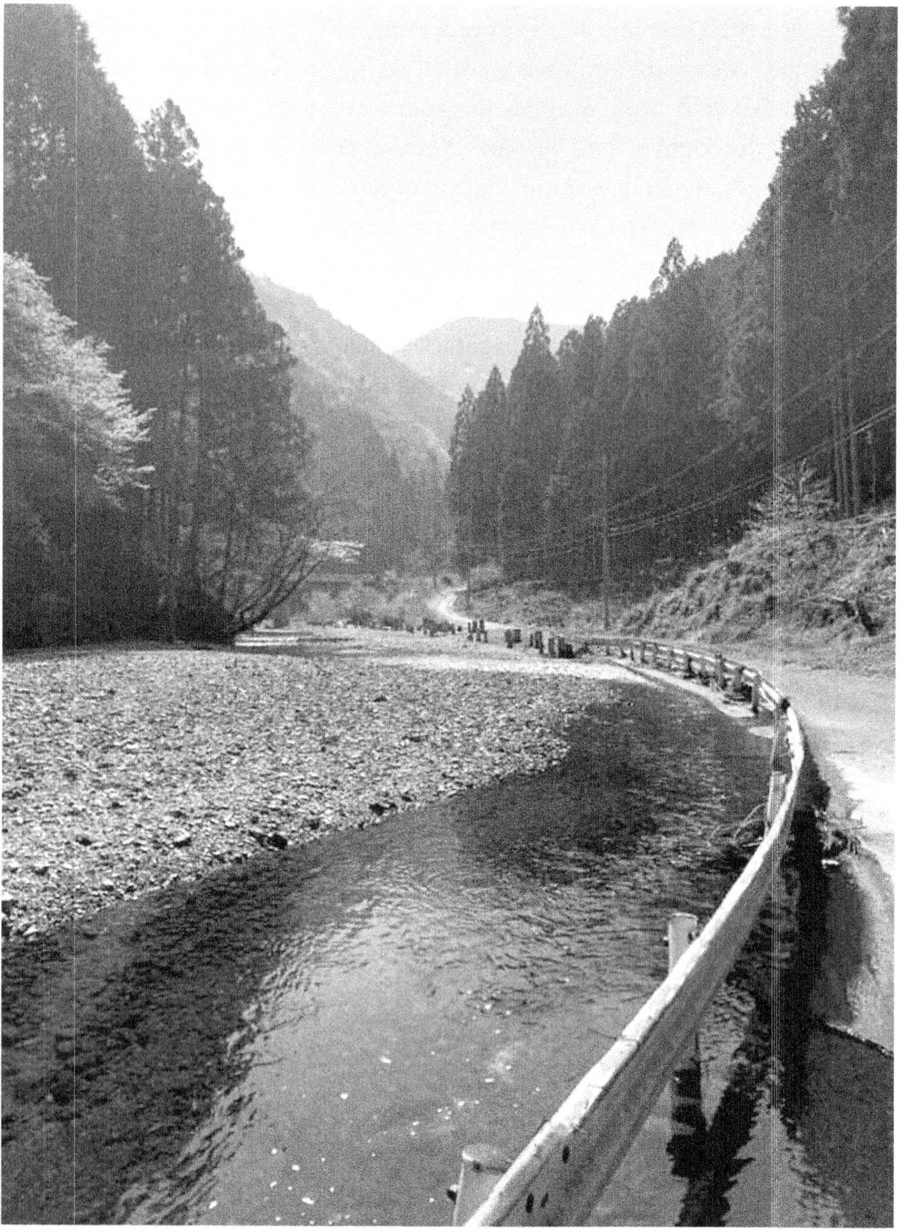

# Peeks on Danger

EDWARD J. TAYLOR

I don't write about my hikes very often. This is mainly because a good number of my friends do it very well on their blogs about Japanese mountains, and serve as far better sources of information than I. But I will make an exception for Minagoyama.

As the pandemic had relieved me of the ability to work, I decided to drive out of town and do two hikes a week, on days with the best weather. It felt like the right time to hike peaks listed on both the Kansai Hyakumeizan and the Kinki Hyakumeizan (a term that can be loosely translated as "100 Eminent Peaks"). As there is a fair bit of overlap between the two, some friends call it the Kinkan 132. Minagoyama is on both lists, a fitting honor for Kyoto Prefecture's tallest peak.

The mountain has no doubt been seen by most visitors to Kyoto, whether they knew it or not. It is most easily identifiable in winter, viewed from the upper Kamogawa riverbank, its snow-covered dome peering over the hills that define the extreme northwest corner of the city.

As I do with many other peaks, I chose a circuitous route, parking near the end and walking up the road to the adjacent trailhead. This usually adds a 20–30 minute slog up a road, so I tried to get it out of the way first. At any rate, traffic was pretty light in those early days of the pandemic.

Leaving the car, I followed the same stretch of Route 367 as I had when I walked the Saba (Wakasa) Kaido, weaving along the older route to avoid tunnels. Luckily this time was without slushy snow. One family had set up a day camp beside the river, and a number of fishermen had staked large sections of water for themselves.

When I reached the trailhead, I found it barricaded and closed off. I presumed that it was the typical overreaction of the local township, in response to one of the many storms we've had over the past few years. Besides, an online resource showed that someone had done this exact route a few weeks before. It wasn't hard to get over the barrier, so up the old forestry road I went.

But I should have taken a hint from all the tumbled hillsides, or the fallen trees. The road eventually ended, my path becoming a series of rock hops across slick boulders where bridges had once stood. More serious were the landslips. Where repaired trails have added ropes or alternate routes around such hazards, here I had little choice but to scramble around, grabbing footholds wherever I could. Most of the time I wasn't that high above the river, but a few sections were pretty dicey. Worst was the lack of trail markers, save for the odd piece of tape here and there. Many of these were on the ground, tied to a fallen tree, so I found myself facing a pop quiz on navigation skills.

Along the way, I pondered why there were so many fallen trees. Throughout history, has this always been the case? I didn't recall this many alterations in hiking routes during my first twenty years of living in Japan. Was it due to increasingly powerful storms? Or perhaps this neglected cedar monoculture had been allowed to grow to such a height that the soil could no longer support the trees' weight, causing them to topple by the dozen in high winds?

Not long after coming to a large Japanese horse chestnut tree, my path made an abrupt right angle. This trail is notoriously difficult, mainly because the final approach to the peak is literally straight up the gully at the stream's end. I grew weary of scrambling from rock to rock, and from treading over debris patches that would have made sound little nests for the vipers no doubt enjoying the same sunshine as I. The slope to the left looked a bit kinder, so I diverted along what looked like the most user-friendly path. This would subtly shift every dozen steps or so, as my eyes got a better sense of the layout. Before long, I was literally hurling myself upward from tree to tree, in order to arrest gravity's pull back down into the ravine.

Then I was on the top. For a few minutes, I was the highest thing in Kyoto prefecture. I sat with my lunch and my guidebook, rolling my eyes when I noted that today's hike was rated the most dangerous out of the 52 within—and that was when the trail had officially been open.

I began the descent, finding some relief in the fact that I was now on well-used trails. But this mountain must be one of the most poorly marked in Japan. I had a choice of three trails down, one of which I wanted to avoid since the map showed hazard marks. It took some doing, but I found my intended trail, a steep drop that required me to use my trekking poles.

At some point the Yamap app I was using showed that I had to make another 90-degree turn down into the next watershed. There was no trail at all, and the pitch was so steep I could no longer remain on my feet. I slid like a baseball player from tree to tree, leg extended in order to brake on the trunks.

Finally I hit the stream, and in my growing fatigue was slightly annoyed that I'd have to rock-hop again. Here, too, storms had left sections in shambles, where I'd have to navigate over big drops down into the ravine. At one point, I stopped cold. Partly buried in the brush of a landslip were a pair of trekking poles with points facing up the hill, beside a hat and a half-empty bottle of tea. Somebody had taken a very hard fall here. It looked as if it had happened long before, but I called out, "Oi, Oi!" a few times, just in case someone was still around. I tried to peer down into the stream below, but I couldn't see too well from where I was precariously perched, and getting any closer would put myself at risk.

I pushed on. At some point the trail leveled off, near an old shack that was half-collapsed back into the forest. I eventually reached the end of my descent, beside a wide, fast-moving river. The bridge I had expected was gone, but I had one final water-crossing to make, moving through currents that pulled strongly at my calves.

Climbing up the far bank, I sat a while beside the logging road that would lead me easily back to my car. There was joy in this final half hour, having come through what I considered an ordeal, but the hike was not finished with me. Later that day, I discussed with a hiking friend my next intended ascent of Minetokoyama, and he cautioned me that its beautiful meadow was notorious for bears. As such, the night before going, I slept poorly, bullied by fear. The high winds of morning gave me the excuse to put off the hike, which brought relief. Then a week later, I faced a similar situation: I awoke at 4:30, and while I'd decided not to go on that day either, over breakfast I essentially said, "Screw it," and just went—and had an excellent day.

I often ponder why I left Minagoyama feeling as I did. I believe that the tracing of two watersheds, not to mention the tree scrambling on the slopes themselves, had triggered a PTSD (Post Traumatic Stress Disorder) of sorts, resuscitating my muscle memory of a near-fatal night on Jyatani-dake, when I'd quickly become disoriented and lost in a sudden blizzard. For the last decade, I've grown more and more afraid of the backcountry, with its ever-present possibility of peril. I don't know if this is part of aging, or a subconscious concern about orphaning my daughter, or (most likely) a larger case of PTSD from the death of my son in the mountains. But the fear is with me much more than before.

So it is that I'll leave the house in the morning, with a furrowed brow, yet I inevitably seem to return with a broad smile.

✻

**Edward J. Taylor** is a writer based in Kyoto. His work has appeared in *The Japan Times, Singapore Straits Times, Kyoto Journal, Skyward: JAL's Inflight Magazine, Resurgence, Outdoor Japan, Kansai Time Out*, and *Elephant Journal*, as well as in various print and online publications. Graduate of the University of Arizona's renowned Creative Writing program, he is a writer for Lonely Planet's *Experience Japan* and now serves as a Contributing Editor at *Kyoto Journal*. Edward is the co-editor of the *Deep Kyoto Walks* anthology, and is currently at work on a series of books about walking Japan's ancient highways.

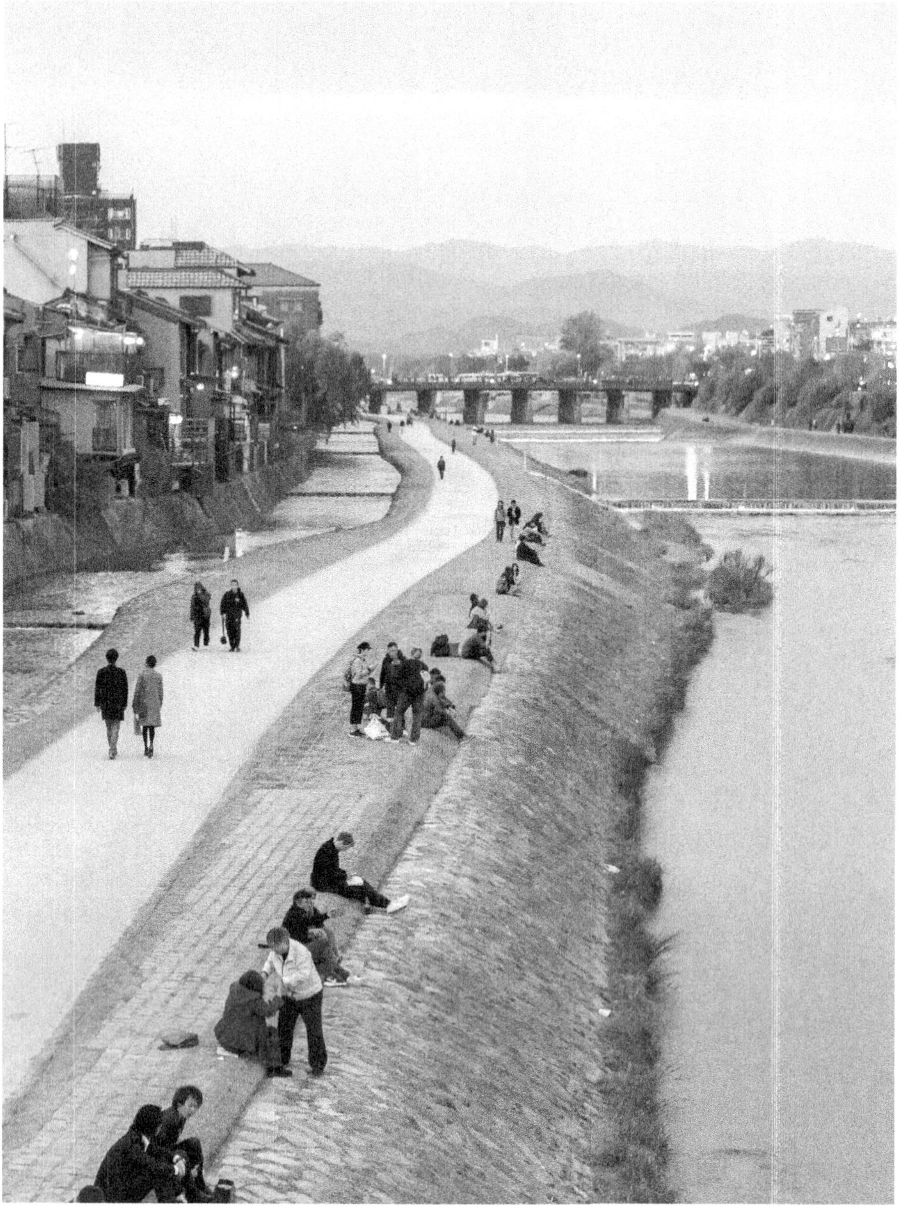

# For the Visitors

FELICITY TILLACK

For we without generations to spare
to understand the *miyabi* of Kyoto,
turn our focus to its outer,
its visible, its surface, its accessible,
its nature.

—

Photographers haunt autumn
inspired by gleaming grasses along the Kamogawa,
*susuki* framed by maples in a car park.
Spot spider lilies in Gosho
before zealous imperial gardeners slice off their heads.
Wander north along Horikawa,
to *shidare* gingko islands,
sunbeam trellises
in slow motion with the wind.
Shuffle across *tatami*,
in turn for a spot
overlooking the garden.

—

Winter's chill seeps down and sticks.
A bath of sliced *yuzu*
in the deep of solstice
might help slough it off.
River banks are beige.
A tin tank of boiled water beneath blankets
ends thoughts of trips outside.
But then, a flurry, a storm, a blizzard.
Traffic stops, cyclists skid, buses don chain mail.
Hike past the mayhem to see
the golden pavilion silhouetted with snow.
Sad pilgrims find that Ryoanji is closed for renovations.

—

Up before buses in flower season,
abandon our bikes by the brickwork.
Above on Keage's quiet tracks
opposing walls of camera colonists,
that arrived long before we,
keep empty a luminescent stretch of cherry blossom blooms,
until a neon jogger breaks the spell.
Macro petals on Philosopher's Path mid-morning;
foreground *sakura mochi*
with Kiyamachi canal bokeh background at lunch;
ride the Randen in the afternoon.
No blossoms?
Took the wrong line, try again.
Selfies while illuminated at night.
Beneath a paper umbrella upload
a million similar shots to Instagram.
いいね！
Tomorrow's forecast says rain.

—

Sunrise at 4:30 in summer.
Take a taxi at 4 to Arashiyama,
enjoy the bamboo grove alone until at least 4:45.
Grandmas hang hydrangeas in the bathroom
to ward off bad *kami*.
Preschool kids with yellow hats and clipboards,
sans teachers,
speed through the Botanical Gardens
trusted to sketch cicada shells.
Their parents prepare *jizo-bon*:
plastic pools for scooping fish,
and mountains of shaved ice.
There is space on the buses again.
Visitors escape the heat.

—

A woman smiles politely at praise for her flowers,
"Come back and see them in another season."
She invites and turns away.
Between the lines,
this conversation is done for now.

*From late summer of 2021, I began a film project at the behest of Robert Weis of Luxembourg National Museum of Natural History. The film was to feature in his exhibition,* The Spirit of Shizen, *in summer 2022, so I would have a year to collect poetic images of Kyoto's four seasons—a year in which international travelers were still blocked from entering the country. I still feel very much a visitor in this ancient city, and I was grateful for the opportunity to capture its most popular destinations without crowds, and uncover corners I might never have visited without this project. The theme of this year's anthology is Nature and as I wrote this poem, I often thought of my experiences making the film. I consider the two to be companion pieces and encourage readers to visit the Luxembourg National Museum of Natural History's YouTube channel to enjoy the film,* The Seasonal Beauty of Kyoto, *and Gianni Donvito's wonderful score.*

※

**Felicity Tillack** is an Australian writer, photographer and filmmaker based in Japan since 2006. Her blog and YouTube channel, *Where Next Japan*, showcases Japan, its culture and lifestyle. She also wrote and directed a feature film, *Impossible to Imagine*, in 2019.

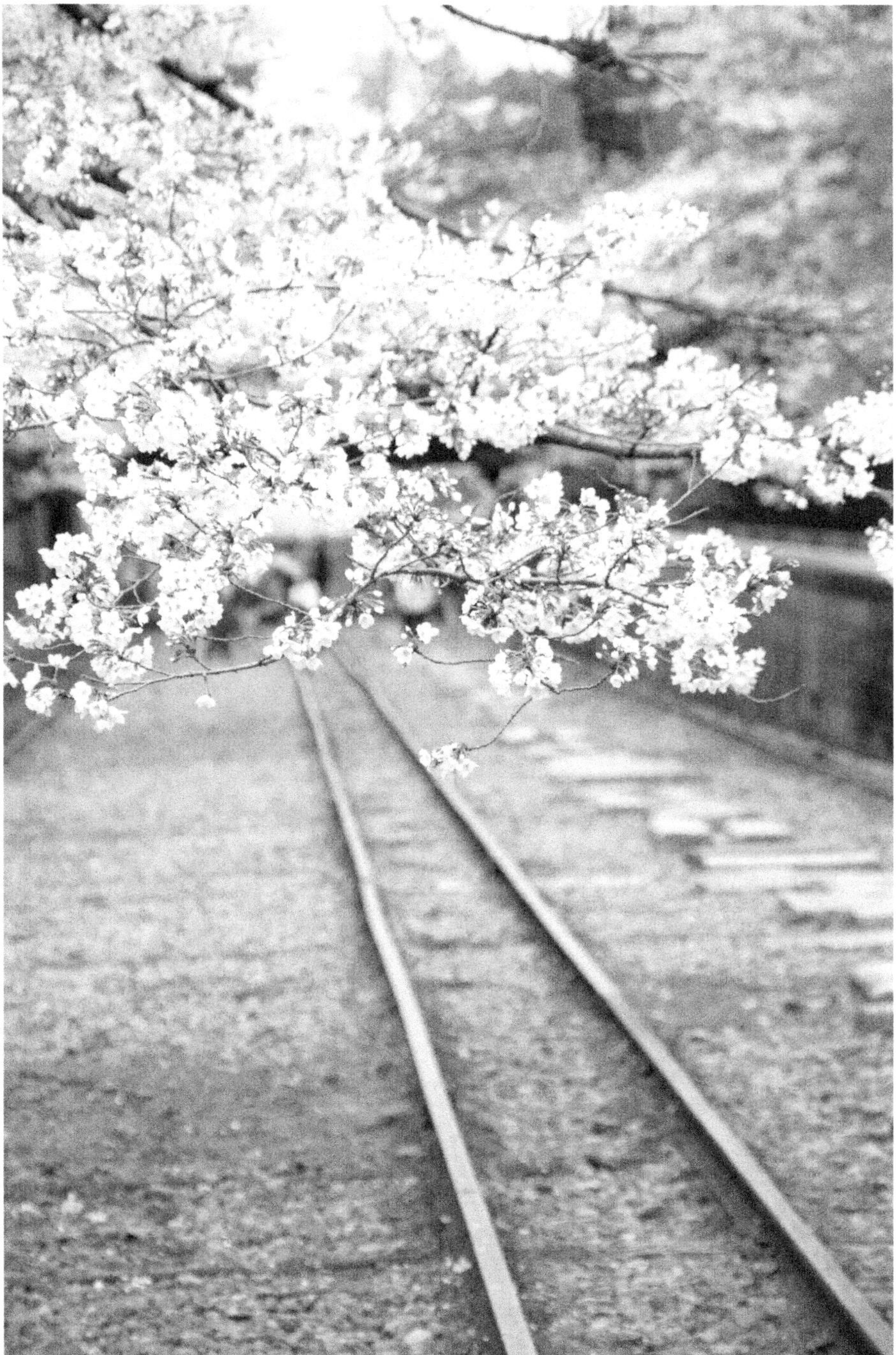

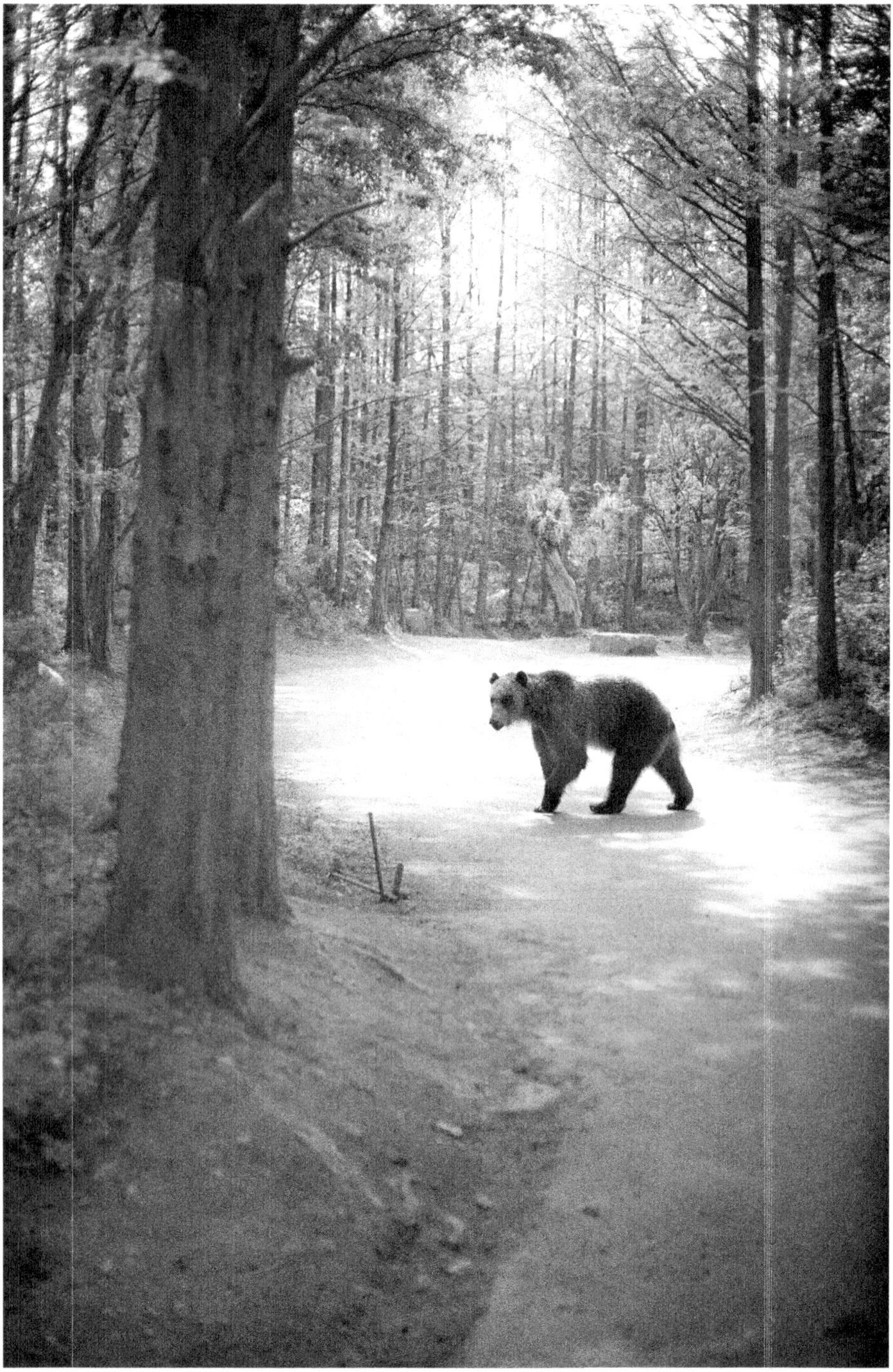

# Nature is Trying to Kill You

FERNANDO TORRES

When most people think about nature in Kyoto, they likely imagine bamboo rustling in the wind like angels' wings, or dragonflies fluttering over the Kamo River. An entire industry has been created to monetize the city's charms. Yet for every natural delight that inspires Zen-like contemplation, there is definitely something out there trying to kill you—and it will do it while you're drinking matcha on the balcony of a hillside temple or pondering the miraculous beauty of nature. Perhaps the time has come to consider the other side of nature in Japan, not merely the yang but the yin.

It was all over the news: a pair of wild boars came down to our neighborhood in Higashiyama and went on a rampage that left five injured. For what seemed an eternity, neighbors and wildlife fought an epic battle of skin, tusk, and teeth. It started with an attack on a high school girl after a mother boar and her child wandered down from the nearby forest, but the real action didn't begin until the beasts ran into an eldercare facility. That's when the ten-minute-long battle, one worthy of a Toei Studios motion picture, started in earnest.

Pity the poor employees who saw the boars enter the facility and decided it somehow fell within their job description to defend their territory. They would soon bear the bites and wounds of warriors; souvenirs they could display as they regaled those fortunate enough not to be present to witness their brave feats. The boars returned to the area and easily won their second round, charging an 81-year-old woman who fell and broke her wrist. A 71-year-old neighbor, a former police officer, decided to enter the fray and put one of the boars in an actual headlock. You'd have to ask why he thought that was a good idea; perhaps he'd been watching too much sumo, but it worked about as well as you might expect. The boar simply bit him and wiggled away. Amid all this mayhem, a steel door was bashed in and splattered with blood, much to the delight of the local news reporters who would later arrive.

That's about the time the carpenter became involved. With the bravery of the samurai who fought here hundreds of years prior, he raised his two-by-four and attacked. Most of the famous duels that occurred during the Muromachi Period were brief: a swift exchange of *katana* blows and one combatant would fall. However, what was about to happen on that quiet Saturday, a few streets from my house, was one of the most heroic duels in the history of Higashiyama. Displaying its thick skin and bristled hair, the boar stared with steely eyes, making clear it was neither fazed nor intimidated by its opponent. The carpenter's *tobi* trousers billowed below his knees, the informal uniform of his trade that emphasized his skill with the board he wielded. For ten minutes, they fought—the carpenter and the boar—and no clear winner emerged, only scars. Nature's battle will perhaps resume at some later time, but for now, the boars wandered back into the hills, and nature's balance was reset.

Needless to say, you won't find any of these incidents in travel brochures, but they happen all the time. There was the boar that injured a bicycle rider at Kyoto University's dorm grounds. And what of the boar that boldly strode into the lobby of the Westin Miyako Kyoto and bit the thigh of a helpless employee? They held it off with a *sasumata*, a type of pole weapon, lest you think my comparisons to the Sengoku period are overwrought. Eventually, the police saved them, but where's Miyamoto Musashi when you need him? Boars have even been seen swimming in Lake Biwa Canal, so don't think that nature isn't getting the upper hand, or at least trying.

I've heard the boars while hiking in the hills near Inari Shrine at night—an unsettling snorting sound from within the shadows, low growls permeating the moonlight's tranquility.

"Run!" I shouted to my friend, but he just stood there and laughed. He had never seen the blood splattered on the punctured metal door from what I now call The Battle of Honmachi. Fortunately, we got away, but he maintained the same blissful ignorance of tourists who feel impervious during their travels.

And what should one make of the "Beware of Monkeys" signs that you find everywhere? Kyoto's municipal government doesn't exactly have the financial wherewithal to put them up without reason. I even escaped being assailed in the hills of Arashiyama by a particularly bold Japanese Macaque pulling at my backpack. Startled, I dove for a slide so long it circumvented a goodly portion of the mountain and slid to safety. Perhaps I should have been on guard as I was still in the general area of Arashiyama's famous Monkey Park, but I had already left the general viewing area. If you're wondering if I told anybody—no, I did not. Pity the poor woman in Shizuoka Prefecture who reported seeing a monkey near Fujikawa Station, only to be accidentally shot in the arm with a tranquilizer gun by those she had called. She dropped to the ground unconscious and had to be taken to the hospital. The monkey got away, presumably laughing as it fled. Recently, nearly forty people were injured in the Yamaguchi prefecture by, presumably, those monkeys' mischievous cousins. Never stare them in the eyes, no matter how cute they might appear, and be especially mindful of any humans trying to wrangle them.

Perhaps you think bears are only something people in Hokkaido need to worry about, except maybe heartburn from some unsavory bear curry? Tell that to the farmer in Fukuchiyama, Kyoto prefecture, who had a bear break into her house and surprise her from behind. The animal fled, but she received hand and foot injuries as she tried to escape. That incident was preceded by over a hundred sightings in the area that year. Nature is out there, and dinner time comes every single day. Signs succinctly warn in English, "You will be savaged by bears." Frankly, I think I'd rather be shot with a tranquilizer dart.

Not too far from Kinkaku-ji, you can find a more appetizing way for nature to kill you. *Fugu* is a basically tasteless fish, but perhaps it's not about the flavor but reminding oneself how it feels to be alive. If I want to feel that, I would simply eat some expired *conbini* sushi. The chefs who make *fugu* are trained professionals and take their craft seriously, leaving just enough poison to slightly numb your lips. This raises the question, why are they leaving any poison at all? Is poison an aspect of *umami* or something? If not, I think I'll pass. Preparing *fugu* is so dangerous that its innards must be stored in multiple bags and special boxes before they're taken to a facility to be destroyed. This system came about because some people were trying to eat it out of the trash and dying. Today, most *fugu*-related casualties come from people preparing the delicacy at home. Around sixty people each year get severe poisoning, with up to six deaths. That's a lot better than the 1980s when around forty people were dying yearly. The lesson? If you are going to battle nature with a fork and knife, be sure to spend years in training or at least pay an expert. Perhaps *fugu* just needs its own city warning signs.

Lest you imagine you will be safe at home, I can assure you that nature is doing its best to find you there and finish its work. Typhoon Jebi ripped off part of the roof of my house, and it injured several people when a glass ceiling collapsed at Kyoto Station. Kansai International Airport closed while I was still in the air, and my flight even made international news. We were somewhere near Russia when a ship crashed into the causeway connecting the airport to land. My plane had to return to Vancouver for another nine-hour layover before departing again for Nagoya, which was as close as I could get to home—and don't even get me started about COVID. I think we all experienced effects from that tussle with nature, but its impact on Kyoto, which relies heavily on tourism and has an aging population, has been particularly severe.

Speaking of home, I was minding my business one day, sitting in my *machiya*'s *horigotatsu*, when a *mukade*—a Japanese giant centipede—rushed for the sunken area where my legs happened to be. Our battle was short, and I came out victorious, but they're not exactly something I had to worry about in California. They're only mildly venomous, but they look like something out of a *kaiju* movie, which is justification enough to reach for my shoe. Apparently, their bite can be quite painful, and I wasn't interested in doing any field research. Sometimes nature just wants to remind you who's in charge.

I'm far more troubled by the huntsman spiders that keep tormenting me. They're even less dangerous than the *mukade*, but no one wants to share their home with a spider the size of a small poodle. The pitter-patter of their legs moving over the *washi* window covers is enough to send chills down the bravest of spines, or even mine. Even more unnerving is how they laugh at my Japanese insect spray, which is apparently less effective than harsh language. Far more dangerous are the redback spiders that have made their way over from Australia, but at least they aren't hairy.

I'm actually more concerned about the murder hornets, as they're often called in the west. These acid-spewing beasts have a higher kill rate in Japan than bears and snakes combined, at around a dozen people yearly. An encounter with the monsters can lead to anaphylactic shock and/or organ failure. I have found three of them inside my house, a result of my handyman leaving the window open for ventilation—but fortunately, all three were dead. Known as *ōsuzumebachi*, or giant sparrow bee in Japan, they can have a wingspan of six centimeters, or at least that's what I've been told. I'm not about to get close enough to take out my measuring tape.

Floods are also a recurring threat in Kyoto, where 260,000 people had to evacuate during Typhoon Man-yi in 2013. Additionally, earthquakes are an ever-present danger, though Kyoto is less susceptible than nearby Kobe, which rests on much less-stable soil. The threat of falling objects is always something to be concerned about, though, and the rumble of a nearby train can put one on edge. I'm from California, so I don't get out of bed unless a quake's magnitude is over 4.8, but I always hope that the large, Meiji-era beam above me will hold.

If you think about it, nature's danger and beauty are consistent with the balance that compels people to appreciate its charms in the first place. That very harmonic dissonance is what resolves within the artist's observations and gives us an appreciation of our place in the universe. Just as the contemplation of death reminds us of the value of life, harmony comes from determining and acknowledging our proper role within its balance. Still, like Jacob wrestling the angel, it is also part of our nature to challenge what cannot be overcome, even as nature is always there to both humble and empower. Nature demands our admiration and respect, and only the fool denies it its dignity. The question is not whether, in fact, nature is trying to kill you, but why?

※

**Fernando Torres** is the author of *A Habit of Resistance*, *More Than Alive: Death of an Idol*, and *The Shadow That Endures*, among other collective works. When he is not busy restoring his 120-year-old house in Kyoto, he enjoys writing music and traveling. Additionally, his symphony celebrating the second edition of *The Shadow That Endures* was recently released on most major streaming services. An instrument-rated pilot, Fernando imbues his writing with the humor and adventure he finds wherever the four winds take him.

WRITERS IN KYOTO COMPETITION | 2021 **THIRD PRIZE**

# Restaurant Boer

HANS BRINCKMANN

In the spring of 1958, I assisted a close friend, Shoko Fujii, in setting up a small Kyoto eatery in Kiyamachi, Shijo-sagaru, in a rented space owned by a gynecologist, right on the narrow Takasegawa. From the options I offered, she chose the name Restaurant Boer (meaning Farmer), the first Dutch restaurant in Kyoto, if not in Japan. It featured smoked eels, hearty soups, and—as the house specialty—very tasty veal-and-bacon rolls known in Holland as "blinde vinken," blind finches. The approximate translation, *mekura-no-suzume*, blind sparrows, sounded so intriguing that we were sure this would guarantee the success of this start-up.

Besides fresh vegetables, they were served with potatoes, *jaga-imo* in Japanese, introduced by 17th century Dutch traders from the Indonesian capital Jakarta, *jagatara* in old-Japanese, thus named *jaga-imo*, *imo* meaning tuber. Other meals were also served, such as cheese dishes and Jachtschotel, a hunter's stew.

But after a brief spell of bookings, customer numbers declined fast, perhaps in part because of the shock caused by the *mekura-no-suzume*, not the taste, but its appetite-destroying name. And the term Boer didn't help either: what was a "farmer restaurant" doing in Japan's sophisticated, ancient capital? The restaurant closed its doors within a year.

But at least there was a happy ending: it was in front of Boer that in October 1958 I was introduced in *mi-ai* style to my future wife, Toyoko Yoshida. Why "in front"? Because although we had planned to meet at Boer, a funeral procession had just crossed the bridge to Boer. "Bad omen!" she called out. "I avoid that bridge!" Instead, I crossed to her side, and from then on, everything went well. We clicked, found common interests, and married four months later. We had a happy marriage.

❋

**Hans Brinckmann** was born in Holland in 1932. Though keen on writing, he joined an international bank. Assigned to Japan in 1950, he stayed 24 years. He returned to Japan intermittently and since 2003 as a permanent resident and writer of seven works of fiction, non-fiction and poetry, including *Showa Japan* (Tuttle) and *The Call of Japan* (Renaissance Books).

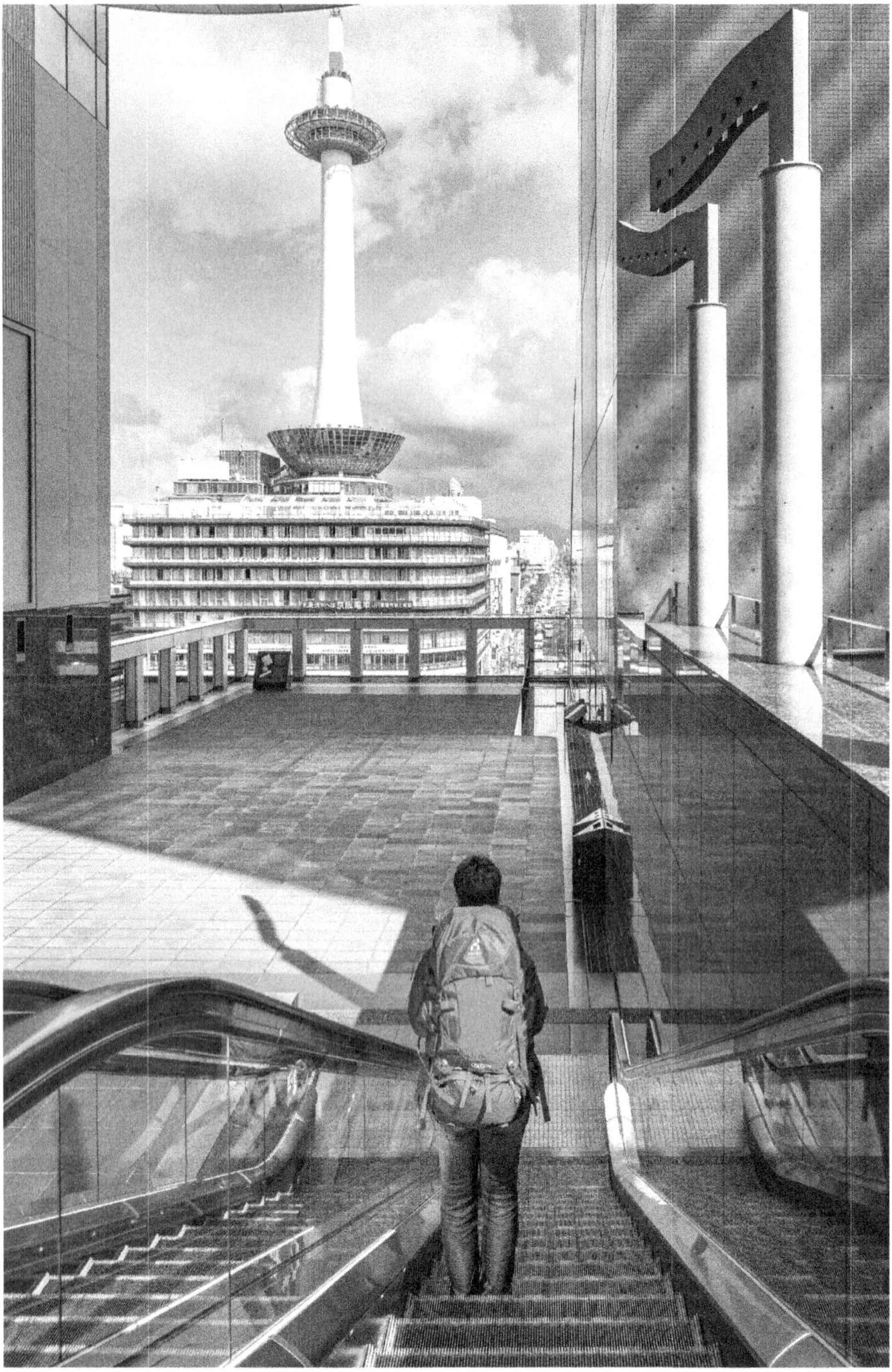

# The Nature of Kyoto: 1006 vs 2006

HAMISH DOWNIE

*After a night of passion, a man hastily wraps his* kosode *garment and slides out the door. Bleary-eyed, he makes haste to his abode, where he must pen a suitable poem of wit and elegance. The walk of shame was made all the worse by this dawning deadline. Not only must he write something for the ages, he must also choose the perfect seasonal piece of flora to accompany the* waka *poem. Otherwise he may be kicked off the cloud of this floating world back into the forgotten farmers of the peaceful age. He spots the fisherwoman's wet sleeves, and he is struck by inspiration: he can make a metaphor about his own sleeves, wet with tears from having to part from his lover in order to pen this prose of love.*

—

After a night of passion, a man slinks out from the one-room apartment of his girlfriend, the one whom only last night he had given the ultimatum: either let me go home with you, or catch the last train and we break up. She was familiar with this routine, but went through the motions of tearfully protesting. The original author of this manipulative play has been lost to time, but its words live on, performed by a certain type of man one sees late at night in train stations, huddled behind some supporting beam or vending machine, as his girlfriend dissolves in a puddle of tears. His act makes any passersby awkwardly feel as if they had intruded on a personal conversation, when in fact this man has thrust this private moment upon the public's blinking gaze, as many of them drunkenly catch their last train home. The following morning, the man's conquest won, he must now depart on the first train, and type out a little message to his girlfriend. He must carefully choose the right words and the perfect emojis to go along with his prose of love, or more likely, his feigned indifference.

—

So much has changed, and yet, so much stays the same. The Heian author Sei Shonangon penned so many delightful lists of places and things, with witty connections, not realising that a thousand years later, the world would be aping her writing style on social media. Her short stories were like today's blogs, and her listicles became today's Buzzfeed clickbait articles. 'Sei Shonangon's 10 Best Lakes in Japan—The Third One Will SHOCK You!'

In 1006, wearing the wrong colours in one's layered *kimono* could lead to banishment and an entry in *The Pillow Book*. Just imagine being written into history because you didn't bathe enough: Sei Shonangon laughed at the plight of another court lady who lifted her *kimono*, only for flies to buzz out from under her garment. We do something similar now, only this time with photographic evidence from paparazzi who snap girls getting out of cars sans underwear — and the public laps it up, crude MS-paint scribblings and all. So much has stayed the same, but without most of the romance and wit.

—

*The Last Snow falls on the first of the Cherry Blossoms,*
*My feet stand in cold slush,*
*Waiting for the taxi,*
*To take me to the hotel to write this terrible poem.*

—

*His sword catches on the* noren *curtain and is confiscated. He's a part-time farmer, and smells like one. He's not the noble warrior that his descendants will be in a couple of eras, but he does have one thing on his side: he eats brown rice and barley, so he's stronger than his opponent, who will only let the most refined white rice pass his lips. The food of kings makes him weak and tired, but the part-time farmer remains jealous, the seed of discontent planted. Soon he will join forces with his brethren and change the* world. The nobleman eyes his muscles with lust, even if his nose is repulsed by the musk of the man he must fight. But first, they share a tea ceremony.

—

The work day bled into a night out at the bar with his work cronies, but the battle has only just begun. His boss is drunkenly holding court, and pointing at one of his subordinates, a recent graduate of one of Kyoto's top universities. Too refined and cultured for the hard battle of sales and business, he's the reason Kyoto is on its path to future bankruptcy. A degree in philosophy doesn't fill one's belly. He chastises the new recruit for costing him money, and encourages him to work harder, and become more like him. The subordinates all agree with their senior, who is paying for their meals.

—

*My love for you is as hot as the Kyoto summer,*
*And it's as true and loud as the stagnant humidity and*
*the humming cicadas*

—

His attempts to craft a poem about his lady friend have all failed. He has only the second half of something, bemoaning the long, dragged-out night of waiting for her to return from her respite in a temple somewhere in the countryside. He sends his boy out to collect his cronies. The rallied troops may help him get his lady back, or at least etch his name into history. He asks them over copious amounts of sake what makes the perfect woman. One states that his wife isn't perfect because she is too cool and refined: when he leaves for a long trip away, she treats the occasion with excessive equanimity. The other crony complains that his wife isn't perfect either, because she cries and gnashes her teeth too wildly, and he wishes she could be more restrained. The conversation goes around in circles until the sun comes up and resolves nothing.

—

I once asked a Japanese female friend to explain to me what made Japanese men tick, and she recommended that I read *Genji Monogatari*, particularly the second chapter. I did, and it confirmed my worst fears: my then-boyfriend wouldn't ever be satisfied by how I acted, whether with the equanimity he demanded, or the passion that he desired and yet also detested. Eventually, many years later, I realised that if you are always too much of something for someone, they probably don't really want you at all. You are just a soft place to land. You don't really have a boyfriend, just a kind of neighbor's cat who occasionally condescends to visit you, eat your food, sleep in your bed, get scratched behind the ears until he purrs…and then moves on to the next house, without giving you a second thought, while you pine away and he judges your passion or lack thereof. Eventually you find a man who is like a dog—not the kind talked about in popular music, but one that acts as dogs really are, loyal and kind and protective.

I am told that it's a big surprise who Genji eventually marries. Sometimes the perfect person doesn't come wrapped up in a predictable package; you may be swiping away true love without even knowing it. True love's smoke signals from across the internet may be misread.

—

*Kyotoites greet the throngs of tourists as warmly as the red maple leaves, but their smiles fall like the dead leaves upon seeing one in the backstreets.*

—

Purists may deride Kyoto's western architecture, and the western hairstyles, but the city is a tapestry of the old and the new. The Matrix terminal train station and the old wooden pagodas nearby are strange bedfellows. Locals-only restaurants whose regulars started going generations ago, and teahouses requiring an introduction to enter, sit next to establishments catering to the tourists who test Japan's *omotenashi* spirit and the specialness of the one-time-only meeting.

Kyoto doesn't bend to the world—the world bends to Kyoto. For example, the logos of global brands have to comply with the city's strict landscaping laws, leading to McDonald's with muted colors instead of the usual garish palette, and the Starbucks nestled in a traditional teahouse. Kyoto is still a floating world, with, but one separate from the rest of Japan; somehow remaining above it, and telling all of us what a nice watch we have, and oh, would we like some *ochazuke* soup? The Emperor and his seat of power may be on loan to Tokyo, but Japan's cultural heart still lies in Kyoto.

—

*Cherry blossoms bloom along The Philosopher's Path, where I sat down and ate a banana sandwich with my mother. The falling petals bring good luck should they land on us.*

※

**Hamish Downie** is an Australian writer/director and ESL (English as a Second Language) teacher based in Osaka, Japan. His debut feature film *Matcha & Vanilla* starring Qyoko Kudo and Tomoko Hayakawa is streaming exclusively on GAGAOOLALA.

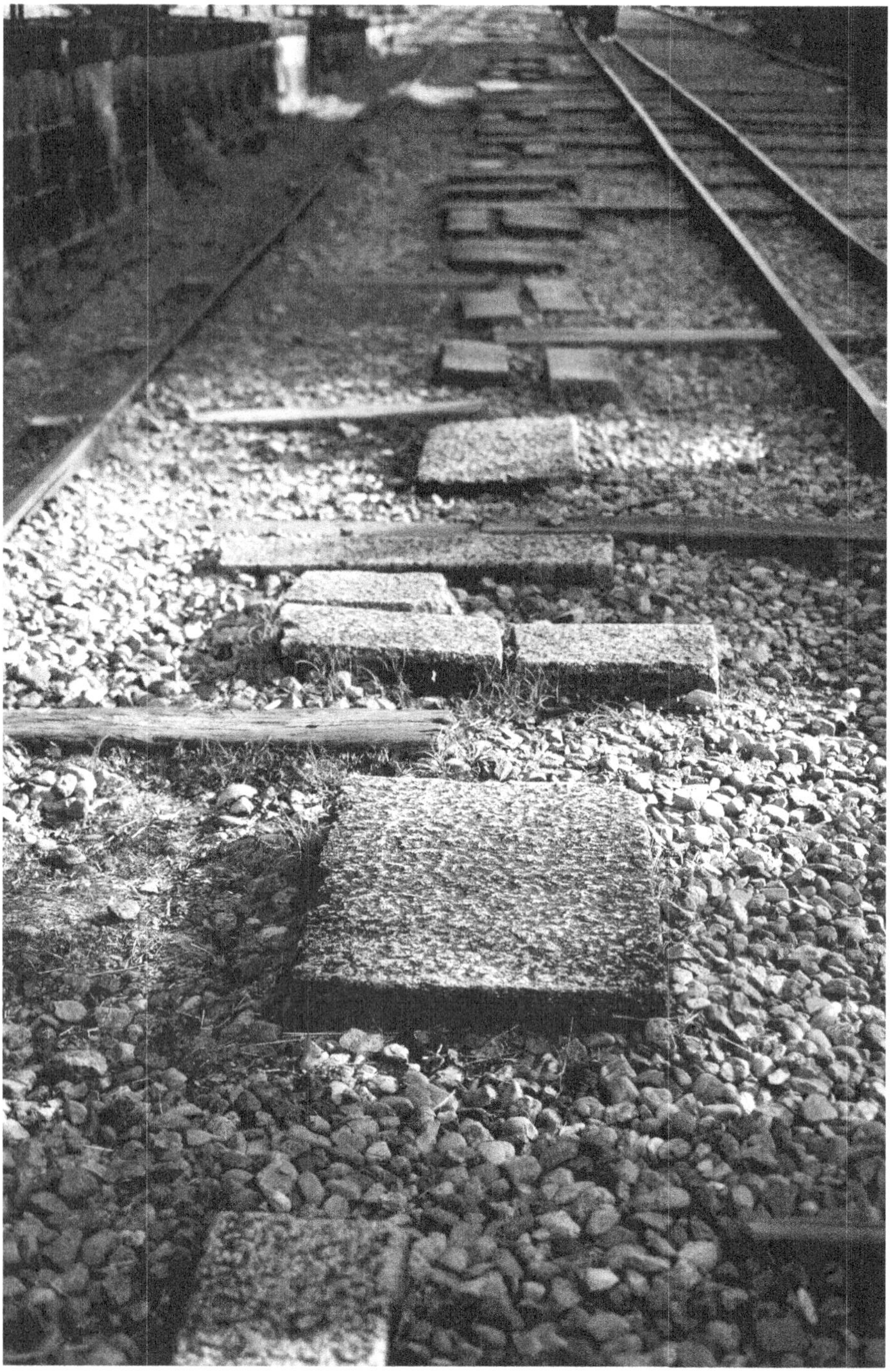

# The Revived Waterway

IRIS REINBACHER

There is something strangely fascinating about abandoned buildings. Maybe it's all the ghost stories that link such ruins to the supernatural. Maybe it is morbid curiosity that compels us to know more about the previous owner of the home and all that's left in it. Or maybe it's a reminder of our own mortality when we see a house overtaken by moss and vines, knowing that eventually, it will succumb to nature, as we all must.

Abandoned hotels, government buildings, and especially factories are even more mesmerizing. We can imagine dozens, even hundreds of lives intertwined with such places—not just the workers, but also people who passed through on errands, or who used the goods produced there.

As far as such industrial ruins go, Kyoto does not have much to offer. Large-scale production facilities, where hundreds of workers toiled away on a single factory floor, never existed in this city dominated by artisans and family businesses. And unused commercial space is repurposed pretty quickly in this town, where the natural boundaries for growth are tight and regulations concerning building heights strictly enforced.

However, there is Keage Incline near Nanzen-ji temple. It's not an old industrial site, but its rusty gates and pipes follow—and occasionally cross—mossy paths and small canals. This is no abandoned factory, even though innumerable goods passed through in its heyday. So, what is it, then? It's one end point of what once was an extremely busy transport route between Shiga prefecture and Osaka. Even today, it remains a power spot of Kyoto, literally.

Let's start at the bottom of the slope. Two pairs of rails start directly out of shallow water, where a little garden of marsh plants has been created and Japanese irises bloom in early summer. The rails lead uphill, and while the top is not far—a mere 500 meters or so—the uneven spacing of the stepping stones makes the climb taxing. During *hanami* season, Keage Incline is one of the most popular and photogenic spots in Kyoto, and it is filled with young people in *kimono*. Most of them stay on the lower third of the slope and do not venture all the way up. Few of them likely know the significance of the rails, and they fail to notice the red brick building that's barely visible on the other side of the road. Further uphill, a sign next to a flat wagon would provide an explanation, but even those who make it that far often ignore it.

At the top of Keage Incline, a little to the left, is a small park with the statue of a young Japanese man in Western clothing. Heian Jingu's huge red *torii* can be seen from there, but people who like abandoned places are more attracted to the large pool of water that temporarily collects in a mossy concrete basin before it noisily disappears in a funnel and rushes downhill, destination unknown.

Further exploration on this side reveals small metal huts of unfathomable purpose, but the warning signs at doors and stairways are unmistakable. Pipes of all sizes appear everywhere, crossing paths, running up and down the huts, beginning and ending at seemingly random places. Enormous twin pipes in green go downhill a short distance before disappearing underground. Maybe these are somehow attached to the funnel in the basin? People brave enough to climb over pipes and follow the water as it flows away in a small canal soon find themselves on a quiet path from which to peek into well-kept temple gardens below. Always outrun by the water, they eventually reach the top of Nanzen-ji's famous aqueduct.

Following the rails instead leads to a pool with an old-fashioned Western-style building on the right. Straight ahead, a tunnel portal can be seen; while unassuming in appearance, it nevertheless conceals on its other side the raison d'être of everything up here, even of Keage Incline itself: The Lake Biwa Canal.

This canal between Otsu and Kyoto was conceived after the Meiji Emperor left for Tokyo, and was meant to help modernize the city and prevent its predicted decline. Built by a Japanese engineer who had just graduated from the Imperial College of Engineering in Tokyo, the canal brought water to the city, channelled through newly-created gardens in Okazaki such as those of Murin-an or Heian Jingu. The water was also used to produce electricity, which boosted textile production in Kyoto and powered Japan's very first electric tram. Finally, the canal provided a much faster way to ship goods from Lake Biwa and the surrounding country to Osaka: aboard countless flat-bottomed boats going back and forth. Keage Incline was the major obstacle on the way. There, the water was rerouted underground to power the turbines in the red brick building on the southern side, leaving the boats on dry land. The steep slope was overcome by loading the boats, cargo and all, onto low rail trolleys, and a system similar to that of cable cars moved them up and down Keage Incline in pairs.

The canal was completed in 1890 after only five years of work. What came as a surprise to everyone at the time was that the new waterway attracted numerous tourists from the moment it was opened. People from all over Japan wanted to see this marvel of modern engineering, with its gently winding canal and three tunnels. Even more sensational was the fact that the entire construction project had been overseen by a team of only Japanese engineers, a novelty at the time. They had been led by 21-year-old Sakuro Tanabe, who was subsequently honoured with the statue in the park on top of the slope. In any case, pleasure boats for tourists soon filled the gaps between commercial vessels.

But nothing lasts forever. Over the years, as rail and road transport became faster than boats, traffic on the Lake Biwa Canal decreased. Operations were finally shut down in 1951. The water from Lake Biwa kept flowing through Kyoto's gardens, and the electricity it generated continued to supply Kyoto's power grid, but the canal and its surroundings went quiet again. Most remnants of the once bustling transport hub were removed, the end of the rails on top of Keage Incline were fenced in for safety, and the gates of the canal's tunnels were shut. The rails on the slope remained but were soon overgrown, and the maintenance required for the water to keep the turbines running in the power station below did not prevent the buildings' deterioration. The stones that formed the canal's bed became mossy without the incessant disturbances of boats passing through, and the slow-running water attracted all sorts of animals. As ever-faster trains were outperformed by private cars, and eventually, by affordable flights, tourists turned to more exotic destinations, and the old waterway beyond the tunnel portal of Keage was largely forgotten.

However, the Lake Biwa Canal remained a popular recreational area for local Yamashina residents. A path for cyclists and pedestrians runs along most of the waterway, and some especially scenic spots provide inviting benches to rest. The dark water flows slowly and attracts herons and ducks, and it is not hard to picture scores of young boys plunging in and learning to swim in the summertime. Spring beckons with white and pink cherry blossoms along most of the canal, and whether the bright autumn colours are more beautiful than the *sakura* is a hotly debated issue in this quiet part of town.

But, nothing lasts forever. After a deep slumber of almost 70 years, the canal opened again in 2018, if only for tourism. In spring and autumn, when the views are especially picturesque, people can experience the wonders and beauty of the old waterway. From one of the boats named after the most current Japanese eras—Reiwa, Heisei, and Showa—it is easy to imagine how life flowed in the Meiji era of 130 years ago, on and around the Lake Biwa Canal.

❋

**Iris Reinbacher** gave up her nomadic life as an academic and moved to Kyoto in 2013. She is now introducing Kyoto's countless daily events on whatsupinkyoto.com. During the pandemic, she spent more time writing than ever. Her piece *Because I Loved Him* on the notorious female killer Sada Abe was published in *The Best New True Crime Stories: Crimes of Passion, Obsession & Revenge*.

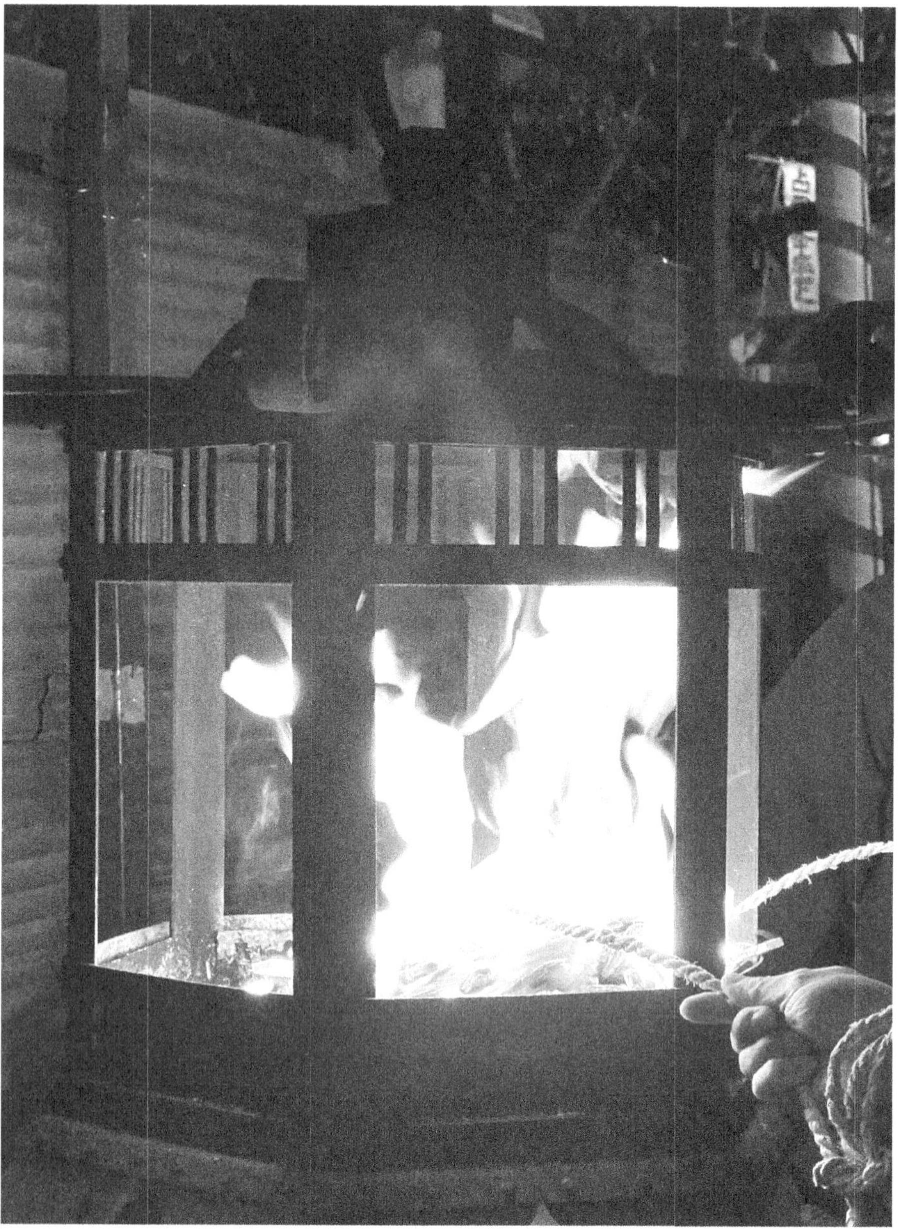

# Kyoto: City of Fire and Water

JANN WILLIAMS

*With fire and water*
 *bursting forth*
  *the newly born year begins*

Ono Emiko, Well-Versed, page 20 (translation by Janine Beichman)

Preparations and rituals associated with welcoming the New Year in Japan are a delight to experience. It is one of my favourite times of year. There are many 'firsts' involved as the year transitions from old to new—the first dream, first sunrise, first look in the mirror and so on. Traditionally there were also 'firsts' associated with fire and water, such as *hatsukamado* (first kindling of the stove), and *wakamizu* (first water, drawn from a well). These were used as seasonal words in *haiku* and have largely become anachronisms with the advent of gas, electricity and piped water. The modern *haiku* by Omo Emiko brings these elements back to life in new form. As described by Minoru Ozawa, who interprets the poem in his book *Well Versed*, by masterfully distilling and simplifying, the poet has evoked the essence of the New Year's kitchen, whose life is (and was) in fire and in water. For me the *haiku* captures the vital energy of these two natural and essential elements.

In Kyoto, many people make the *wakura-mairi* pilgrimage to Yasaka Jinja in Gion on New Year's Eve. There they transfer *okera-hi*, a sacred fire, to a fire rope made of bamboo. *Okera* refers to the medicinal herb *Atractylis ovata*, which is believed to cast away the evil energy of the past year and to bless people with longevity. The ritual originally took place in early February according to the lunisolar calendar used in Japan. The move to the end of December occurred after the Gregorian calendar was introduced in 1873. Traditionally the burning rope would be taken home to cook *zoni* (mochi soup) in the New Year and to light the altar candles to pray for good health and good fortune throughout the year.

On the eve of the Year of the Water Rabbit (2023), I took part in the contemporary form of this tradition. My 'fire rope' was lit in a sacred flame burning in a lantern. It was exciting to see people continuously swinging the ropes to keep the fire alight. Today, the extinguished fire rope, or a limited-edition version from Yasaka Jinja, can be displayed in the kitchen as a fire prevention charm.

The fire rope from New Year's Eve is proudly displayed in my small kitchen in Kyoto, opposite another powerful fire charm from Mt. Atago. The mountain has been associated with fire protection in Kyoto for centuries and has a fascinating history involving *yamabushi* (mountain ascetics) who spread the fire cult across many parts of Japan. Every year on July 31st it is possible to climb Atago-san at night to pray and buy fire-protection charms to put in the kitchen. In 2019 I joined thousands of people who made the long ascent to participate in the Sennichi Tsuyasai fire festival (the 'one thousand days all night festival') at the top of Mt. Atago. Undertaking the 1,000-day pilgrimage (Sennichi Mairi) is believed to grant a thousand days of protection from fire-related disasters and a thousand days of flame for cooking and heating. It was very hot, very humid and very invigorating being able to participate in this sacred, mystical event. In 1987 Anne-Marie Bouchy published a seminal paper on the religious history of Atago-san, including the major changes instigated by the Meiji Restoration of 1868. Like Yasaka Jinja, prior to that period the site combined Buddhism and Shinto, with a strong Shugendo presence on the mountain. This association is being revived and I have gratefully joined two pilgrimages there with the Wani-Ontakesan Shugendo community.

The concern about fire protection in Kyoto stems from a history of major conflagrations that have transformed the city numerous times. Notably, much of Kyoto was destroyed during the Onin Wars (1467–1477) and again during the Great Tenmei Fire in 1788. According to records from the time, the 1788 fire engulfed 36,797 houses (equivalent to 65,340 families), 201 Buddhist temples and 37 shrines. It was noted in the official record book of a high-ranking Dutch officer in Deijima that 'people are considering it to be a great and extraordinary heavenly portent'. The Imperial Palace and Nijo Castle were also destroyed, including the Keep. Unlike the Imperial Palace, it was not rebuilt. Nijo Jinya, located close to Nijo Castle, survived the 1788 fire—one of the few structures that did. It has several built-in fire prevention measures, in addition to its possibly more famous *ninja*-style security features.

The last Great Fire in Kyoto occurred in 1864, the consequence of a rebellion against the Tokugawa Shogunate. The Ofunehoko Gion float restored in 2014 was destroyed in this fire. The large dragon head was added to the float in 2019 after a suitable reference was found, and gilded in 2021. The main hall of Daihoonji (aka Senbon Shakado) remarkably escaped all the large fires and was designated a National Treasure for its rare early architecture. Built in 1227, it is the oldest in Kyoto. In contemporary times the red fire buckets in the backstreets and temples and shrines in Kyoto, the night-time community patrols in winter where wooden clappers and the call '*Hi no Yojin*' ('Beware of Fire') attract attention, fire prevention posters and fire prevention week in November all serve as reminders to Kyotoites to beware of, and have a healthy respect for, fire.

Like fire, water is an element that is both feared and revered. The pure water in the many springs and wells in and around Kyoto have long been associated with *sake* brewing, the tea ceremony, *tofu* making, and fine cuisine. Matsuno'o Taisha in the foothills of western Kyoto, Kiyomizudera in the eastern foothills, and Kifune Jinja in the northern mountains have long associations with water as a sacred entity. Like fire, water is widely used in purification rituals in Kyoto. Like fire, water has caused damage, in this case through the action of floods.

Rivers have been regulated and rerouted from at least the sixth century when the Hata clan, immigrants from Korea, are believed to have constructed weirs on the Katsuragawa in western Kyoto. Large-scale engineering projects have been a feature of water management in the city ever since. When Heian-kyo (Kyoto) was established at the end of the eighth century, the course of the Kamogawa (Kamo River) was altered to flow east of the palace, waterways were channelised and ponds created. Massive flood-control projects were undertaken in the late 1500s in the Uji River and Lake Ogawa when Toyotomi Hideyoshi constructed Fushimi Castle. Around 1611 the Takasegawa canal was built next to the Kamogawa for transportation purposes, and it contributed to strong economic growth. In the 1870s the construction of the Lake Biwa canal saw Kyoto become the first city in Japan with electricity. Water flowing along concrete channels is still a feature in contemporary Kyoto. Humans have transformed the nature of the city's water dynamics and fire has transformed the nature of its look and layout. Both are essential elements in the creation of the Kyoto we know today.

Dragons (*ryu*) are an integral part of the story of fire and water in Kyoto. These mythical creatures are found dispensing water at the *temizuya* (purification basins) of temples and shrines; carved on temples and painted on their ceilings (principally Zen); associated with rain-making ceremonies for over 1200 years ; respected as Kurikara ryuo, a personification of the Wisdom King Fudo Myoo and as an incarnation of Kannon; and painted on jackets related to fire-fighting during the Edo period (and sometimes tattooed on the bodies of fire-fighters themselves). Importantly, dragons are one of the four guardian animals (*shishin*) that protect Kyoto and played a role in the founding of the city. The dragon is often paired with the phoenix, the guardian animal that represents fire and the southerly direction. The mythical creature is also paired with the tiger, representing yang and heaven, and yin and earth respectively.

One of the legends of Yasaka Jinja describes a pond underneath the main shrine known as the 'dragon hole' where the Blue Dragon (Seiryu which protects the city in the east) lives. The underground streams associated with the pond are said to continue toward Shinsen'en in the west where the dragon deity Zennyo Ryo resides. *Goshuin* (sacred stamps) I have collected at both Yasaka Jinja and Shinsen'en feature dragons. A festival is held at Kiyomizudera, also in the eastern foothills, in spring and autumn each year to celebrate the legend of the Blue Dragon and welcome the season. The dragon is said to drink from the Otowa waterfall at the temple. The sutra-covered guardian dragon paraded in the festival was designed by the Academy Award-winning costume designer, Emi Wada, a Kyoto native. Additionally, a large permanent statue depicting dragons is found at the entrance of the west gate of Kiyomizudera. A dragon's den is also found under the main shrine of Kifune Jinja to the north.

Dragons are overwhelmingly associated with the element of water in Japan, as well as being a protector of Buddha and bringers of the rain of Dharma. Protection of buildings from fire is also afforded by dragons as described at Daikakuji, a Shingon temple in Arashiyama, where a dragon is painted on the ceiling of Yasuido. Better known are the large dragons painted on the ceilings of a number of Zen temples in Kyoto. The NHK Core Kyoto documentary *The Dragon: Deity of Water, Protector of the Capital*, released in December 2022, introduces three spectacular Zen ceiling dragons. It notes that since ancient times people in Kyoto have had an affinity with dragons and their invisible energy still imbues the ancient capital today.

The sacred nature of fire and water in Kyoto—and more broadly in Japan—is undeniable. Their use in purification rituals in Shinto, Buddhist and Shugendo ceremonies and festivals abound in the ancient capital. *Goma* (fire) rituals are a striking feature of Esoteric Buddhism and Shugendo practice. The cyclical nature of life that needs constant regeneration as it moves between the forces of pollution and purification, death and rebirth imbue many rituals. The Gozan no Okuribi ('5 mountains send-off fires') is an annual Kyoto ritual in which fires lit on the mountains help deceased souls find their way back to the Other World. Held on August 16th during Obon, the Daimonji is the most recognisable character set alight. It is a spectacular sight. The annual fire festival held on October 22nd at Kurama, in the mountains north of Kyoto, is also justifiably famous. Here the numerous fire torches and bonfires facilitate the spirits' journey to Yuki Jinja, reenacting a procession held over 1,000 years ago when the shrine was moved from Kyoto to Kurama to protect the city's northern quarter.

The elements of fire and water are often paired, having yang and yin characteristics respectively. Their importance and influence in Kyoto are intimately interconnected. As Emiko's *haiku* conveys, together these elements bring life to the kitchen. Fudo Myoo, with his halo of flames, is often associated with waterfalls. Morihei Ueshiba, the founder of Aikido, described Kami as a mnemonic for the interchange of Fire (*ka*) and Water (*mi[zu]*). He taught that the exchange of the cross of Heaven/Fire/Water/Earth gives rise to all things in the universe. Ueshiba-sensei was strongly influenced by Oomoto, a Shinto sect based in Kyoto Prefecture. Here he developed the spiritual vision that permeates the ethical framework of Aikido.

Eikando, a Jodo Shu temple in the eastern hills of Kyoto, offers a different perspective on fire and water in a spiritual context. The parable of the Two Rivers and a White Path is strikingly represented in the Shakado Hall by paintings donated by Sekiguchi Yuki (1923–2008). I came across the imagery in 2022 when viewing the fiery autumn leaves for which Eikando is famous. The turbulent river of water on the left side of the hall represents greed and lust, and the pulsating river of volcanic fire on the right represents fury and hatred. Fire and water are said to represent two of the three poisons or innate human flaws that cause us pain and hinder the path to enlightenment. By single-mindedly following the narrow white path between the two rivers, guided by Amitabha Buddha, the man in the parable safely reaches the other side and is saved from the perils of fire and water. The Fire-Warden Amida, said to have escaped the fires of the Onin War, is also found at Eikando.

The nature of Kyoto: wherever you explore, a city of Fire and Water awaits.

*References:*

Bouchy, Anne-Marie (1987) The Cult of Mount Atago and the Atago Confraternities. *The Journal of Asian Studies*, 46: 255–257.

Ozawa, Minoru (2021) *Well-versed: Exploring Modern Japanese Haiku*. Translated by Janine Beichman. Japan Publishing Industry Foundation for Culture.

Wikipedia (sourced January 2023) for the quote by the Dutch officer in Deijima; and japanese-wiki-corpus.org for the statistics related to the Great Tenmei Fire.

Williams, J. (2019) Shinsen'en: a Heian-kyo Power Spot. In: Williams, J. and Yates, I.J. (Eds) *Encounters with Kyoto. Writers in Kyoto Anthology 3*. pp. 57–65.

※

**Dr. Jann Williams** is an award-winning ecologist, writer, editor and photographer who lives in Tasmania, Australia and is a frequent visitor to Japan. In 2019 she was presented the prestigious Gold Medal of the Ecological Society of Australia and was chief editor and designer of *Encounters with Kyoto*, the third Writers in Kyoto Anthology. Since mid-2022 Jann has taken on the role of Anthology Supervisor for the group. Her blogs, *Elemental Japan* (www.elementaljapan.com) and *Fire up Water down* (www.fireupwaterdown.com), share her unique experiences and insights exploring nature's elements in Japan and around the globe.

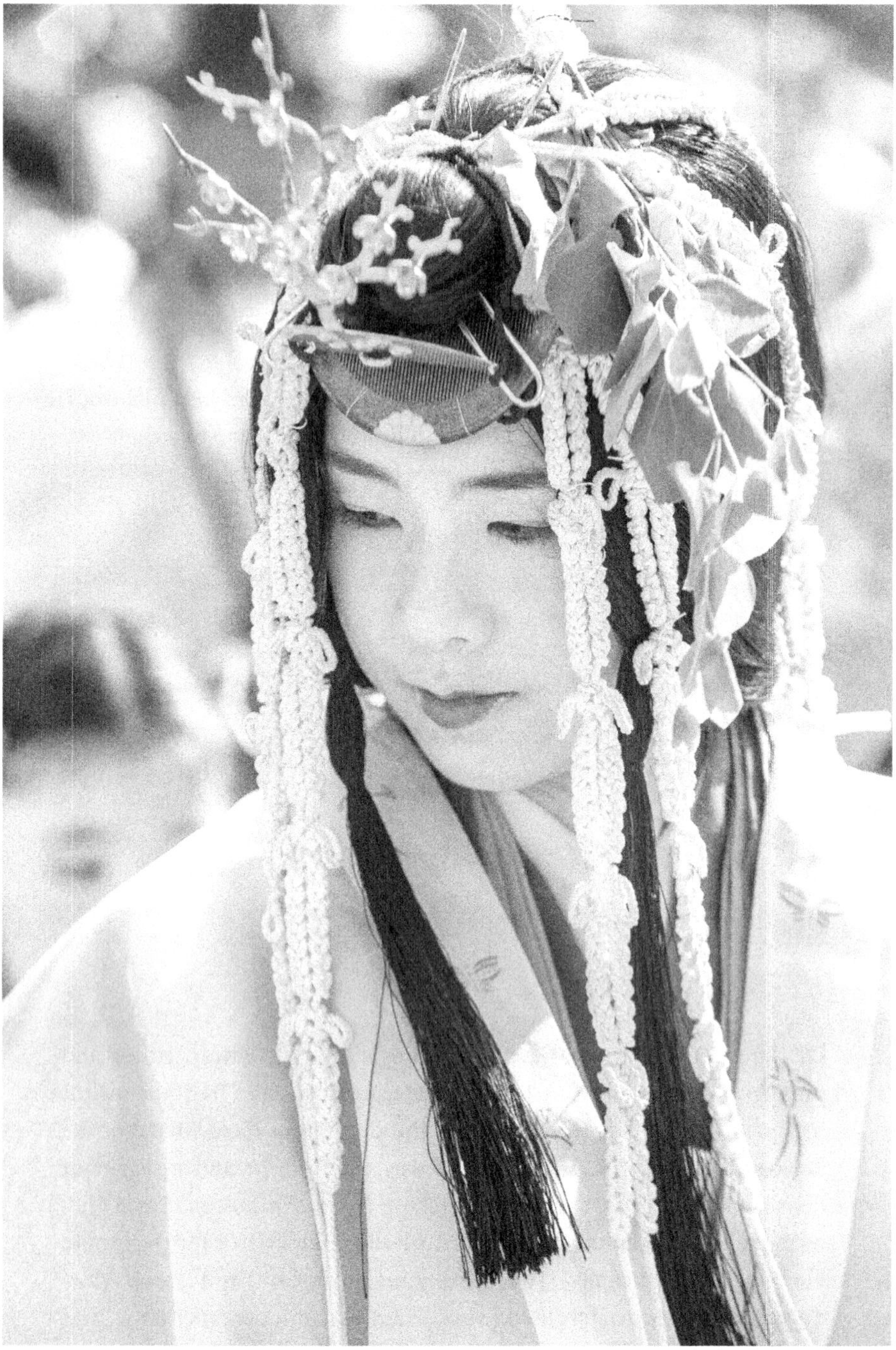

# Vignettes

JOHN DOUGILL

**Sunrise**
Sleepless, I step out onto the veranda to view the 36 peaks ranged along the Eastern Hills. Yellow streaks spread out from Daimonji, like a halo, its almost horizontal top silhouetted against the imperceptibly brightening sky. Daytime pushes darkness ever further west, and in the south, patches of blue appear amid the clouds. Overhead, shafts of light break through the canopy, and to the north, the sky takes on an undercoat of orange. Halfway between Mt Hiei and Daimonji, a white orb appears, so lustrous it hurts the eyes. A solitary ray kisses the paper *shoji*, moving upwards like a lover caressing the neck of his inamorata. Unseen, the little Eiden train rumbles towards *tengu*-haunted Kurama, and as it moves beyond earshot, the shrill of insects resumes. Too late and too chilly for cicadas, it is the season for crickets.

As the Eastern Hills deepen into purple, befitting an imperial city, a golden glow spreads over Kyoto. A new day dawns on Japan's ancient capital.

\*\*\*\*\*\*\*\*\*\*\*\*\*\*\*\*\*\*\*\*

**Midday**
Gentle breeze
Flowers swaying
A stronger gust
Branches bend —
Invisible force
Catches attention

Small birds
Bustling
Wings that flutter
Trembling twigs —
The chatter
Evokes a smile

Wind and birds
River ever-flowing —
Heian to Heisei
The blessings of nature

*********************

### Imadegawa Bridge

A sunny Sunday. Open sky, flowing water, abundant greenery. Cyclists stream along the tree-lined river banks, dog walkers emerge for evening assembly.

To the north, the confluence of Kamo- and Takanogawa marks Kyoto's power spot, two streams of energy sanctified by the ancients with the foundation of a prestigious shrine. Full well did they know the geomancy, and still today the area is crowded with young and old, drawn by the spirit of place.

It is possible to see in the layout of the shrine, located in woodland, the setting for symbolic rebirth. Viewed from above, the pathway and clearing resemble the shape of a womb. The Japanese word for the approach—*sando*—is a homonym for the birth canal, and the vaginal entrance through the *torii* leads to the holy sanctum where 'fertilisation' takes place. In this way 'new life' is generated through the meeting of the vertical (descent of the spirit) with the horizontal (arrival of the worshipper). In the meeting of the two is generated renewal, which is so central to Shinto. Like other post-shamanic cultures, it cherishes the life force, as a result of which the whole country was once covered with fertility symbols.

In the generative triangle where the rivers conjoin, a student party is taking place, with guitars and high spirits. Under the bridge, someone is practising ukulele. Couples sit at regular intervals along the grass verge, and children hop between concrete turtles set in the shallow waters of the river flow. A group of young men wade knee-deep upstream, while overhead, kites soar in predatory manner, eyeing the food being consumed by picnickers.

As daytime darkens, people head for home. Under the bridge, city council panels depict paintings from the seventeenth century showing the pleasures of the riverside. The attire is different, but the enjoyment is the same.

Plus ça change…

\*\*\*\*\*\*\*\*\*\*\*\*\*\*\*\*\*\*\*\*

**Now hear this**
One of the reasons Lafcadio Hearn loved Japan was the delight taken in insect sounds, appreciation of which was refined by the aristocrat-aesthetes of Heian-kyo. The steady drip of raindrops in the rainy season, the cicada in the summer heat, the gurgling of spring streams from melting snow—such was the stuff of poetry. Discerning listeners today can still hear distinctive sounds that evoke the city of yesteryear: temple bells that boom at the end of day, *geisha* singing *kouta* in an old wooden house, Zen monks on their begging rounds.

One of the most characteristic Kyoto sounds is water boiling in the tea ceremony. Guests sit motionless on bent legs as the kettle builds up steam, followed later by the whisking of the tea. The ceremony took shape and was regulated in Kyoto, which contributed the purity of the water drawn from the huge lake that lies beneath the city.

Another treasured sound is that of the bamboo groves, which provide visual delight in their tall trunks and filtered sunlight. The wind rustling through the leaves is celebrated for its '*zawa zawa*' sound, while the creaking and groaning of the slender stems speak to their famed flexibility.

However, the ultimate Kyoto sound lies underground. Imagine a temple garden. You place your ear against a bamboo pipe protruding from the earth, and for a moment there is nothing but a profound silence. All of a sudden a startling sound reverberates, as if from deep within a chamber. As it merges back into nothingness, there comes a sense of calm. Here is the auditory equivalent of the dry landscape garden, each drop a rock in an ocean of emptiness. Just as the stone basin holds water for physical cleansing, the sound of the *suikinkutsu* purifies the soul. It represents acoustic aesthetics at its most sophisticated.

\*\*\*\*\*\*\*\*\*\*\*\*\*\*\*\*\*\*\*\*

## Haibun

For two complete cycles of the Chinese zodiac, I've walked the banks of the Kamogawa. Sometimes it sparkles with joy beneath cherry-bordered blossoms; sometimes, parched and litter-strewn, it limps along like a bedraggled dog. Today, in the late summer sunshine, it basks as contentedly as the pigeons nestled in the nearby grass. It seems all nature has time to spare, none more so than the long-necked egret peering motionless into the distance. Was Murasaki Shikibu entranced by such a scene 1,000 years ago? Did poets of old sit on this rock, also struggling for the elusive word? Opposite me, the thatched study of Rai Sanyo looked over semi-rural views, inspiring him with notions of 'crystal streams and purple mountains'. I close my eyes and let the gentle sound of flowing water wash over me...

>Ascending, soaring
>Beyond the blue horizons
>The lone hawk

*********************

## Aoi Festival

On May 15 every year the oldest of Kyoto's Big Three Festivals takes place. The Aoi Matsuri is the city's spring event; the Gion Matsuri is the summer bonanza; and the Jidai Matsuri is the autumnal offering. In winter there is a break to enjoy Oshogatsu (New Year) festivities.

The festival originated in the sixth century in a desire to please the *kami* and prevent disasters. Nowadays, over 500 people participate in Heian era costume, as well as 36 horses and two ox-carriages. The procession starts from the Former Imperial Palace, and the stately progress means that it takes an hour to travel the short distance to Shimogamo Shrine.

All the gorgeous aesthetics of Heian aristocratic society are on display. The headdress of a court lady is suggestive of the shamanic *miko* of ancient times. Like others in the procession, she wears the emblematic *aoi* leaves, thought to protect against the plague. (Usually translated as hollyhock, *aoi* is in fact closer to wild ginger.)

The procession stretches out to become half a mile long, consisting of horseback warriors, foot soldiers, courtiers, lower-rank guards, higher-rank nobles, halberd bearers and dignitaries. At Shimogamo, dances are performed for the *kami* and the imperial messenger delivers greetings. At 2:20 the procession sets off for

Kamigamo Jinja, where it arrives after two hours, and rituals are again performed.

In medieval times, there were two processions, one for the imperial messenger proceeding from the Imperial Palace and the other for the Saiin (an unmarried female related to the emperor and appointed as titular head of the shrines). Between 810 and the early thirteenth century, when the practice fell into abeyance, there were 35 such priestesses who lived in palaces located somewhere between the two Kamo shrines.

In former times the procession of the Saiin would meet up with that of the imperial messenger, and they would proceed together to the shrines. Nowadays everyone sets off from the south side of the Former Imperial Palace, and the role of the Saiin is played by an unmarried female from a local family of high social rank. Should it rain, the whole event is postponed. After all, the exquisite costumes, which include the *junihitoe* (twelve-layered ceremonial *kimono*), were not intended to serve as rain-gear.

Heritage, memory, animism, the connections of human and place—Kyoto's oldest festival represents all that is best in the Japanese tradition. By honouring the past, the country asserts its identity and looks to the future.

\*\*\*\*\*\*\*\*\*\*\*\*\*\*\*\*\*\*\*\*\*

### Sunset at Shogunzuka

Here is where it all began, the quest for perfection, here at Shogunzuka. Here it was that Emperor Kammu stood and assessed the lay of the land. A mountain in the northeast to keep out evil demons. Encircling mountains to provide protection, with plentiful provision of water and wood. Open land to the south to enhance the energy flow. Here, it is said, he buried a *shogun* statue under a mound to protect his future capital.

According to tradition, in the year 794, on the second day of the 10th month, Emperor Kammu stood on this hillside and surveyed the river basin below. 'The mountains and rivers are the collar and belt of this area and make it a natural citadel,' he declared. It was to be the location of his new capital, Heian-kyo.

Still today the site offers commanding views. From the observation deck, one can even see Osaka to the south. Best of all are the stunning sunsets over the western hills. Could Kammu ever have imagined the glorious future of his foundation, fostering the bond of human and nature on which artists and craftsmen would draw for their creativity?

※

**John Dougill** founded Writers in Kyoto in 2015, since which time membership has risen from seven to seventy. He also runs the *Green Shinto* blog, which in 2011 was the first of its kind. For over twenty years he taught British Culture at Ryukoku University, becoming Emeritus Professor on retirement, and he has written over 25 books. Four of them are about Kyoto in particular: *Kyoto, A Cultural History* (OUP/SIgnal); *100 Kyoto Sights* (Tuttle); the co-authored *Kyoto, A Literary Guide* (Camphor Press), and with photographer John Einarsen *Zen Gardens and Temples in Kyoto* (Tuttle). He was also chief editor of *Echoes* (2017), WiK's second anthology.

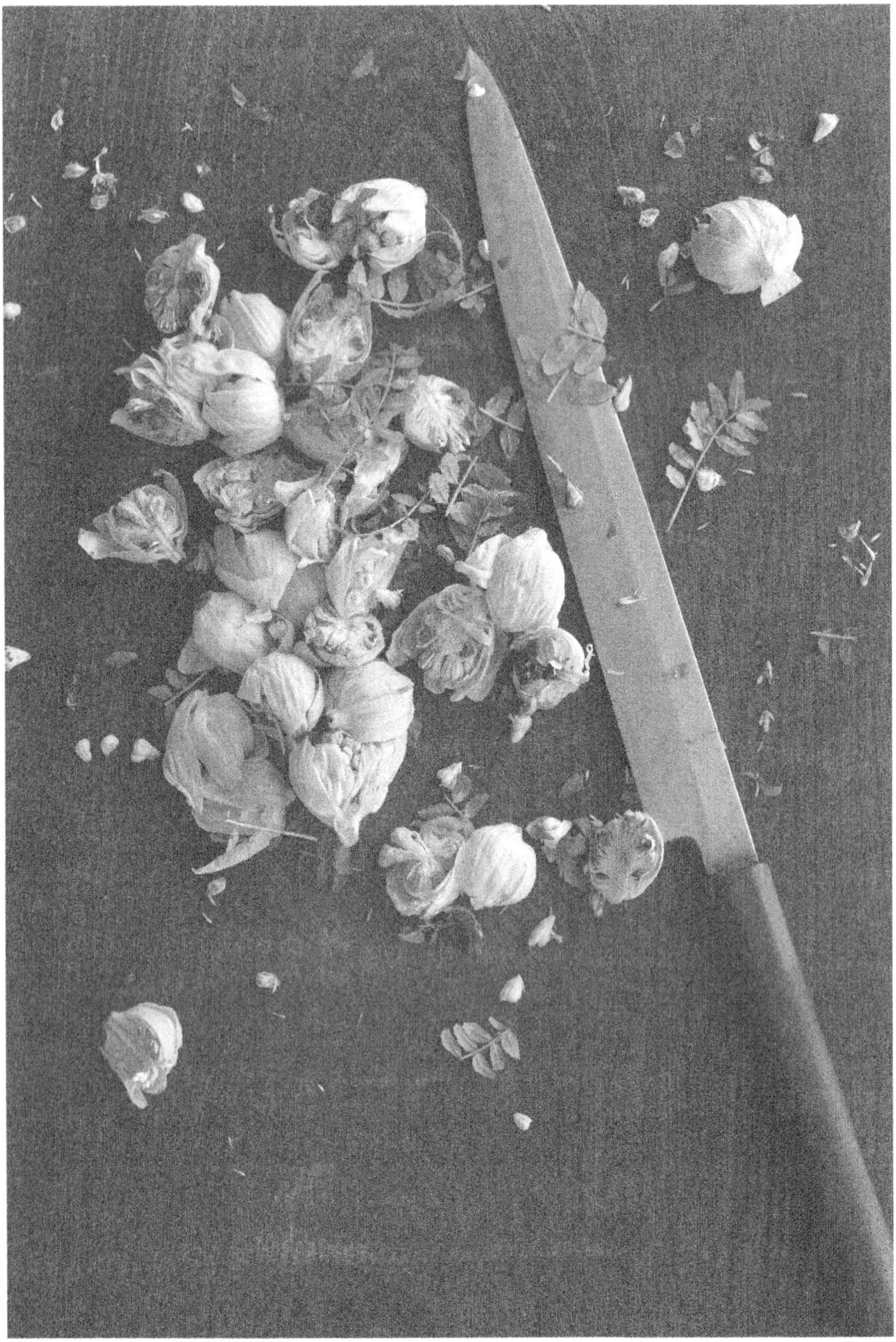

# Food for Thought and for the Thoughtful

JULIAN HOLMES

Kyoto Prefecture is blessed with a relatively temperate climate and abundant rainfall. Its weather is quite predictable—mild winters and hot, humid summers, and a large temperature difference between day and night. This makes Kyoto's climate ideal for growing vegetables, and farmers around the city produce a wide variety. Thanks to the city's relatively small size, restaurateurs can easily drive out in the morning to stock up on the freshest and most delicious of ingredients that nature has to offer.

If you live in Kyoto City for even a short while, you will find that its calendar is heavily influenced by the seasons and revolves around food. Chefs fill their menus with seasonal dishes featuring the very best local produce. It is no exaggeration to say that you can literally tell the time of the year by the vegetables served in front of you. This 季節感—"sense of the seasons" or "seasonal culinary aesthetic," as I would call it—features very prominently in Kyoto cuisine.

There are always vegetables in season and dishes to look forward to all year round. This makes Kyoto a gourmet's paradise, which is why its restaurants are popular with its residents and visitors alike.

Despite being Japan's ninth largest city, Kyoto is not so big. As of 2022, its population stood at a mere 1.46 million. In pre-pandemic years, this figure was dwarfed by the number of visitors to the city. According to the Kyoto Municipal Government, the number of visitors staying overnight in 2019 was 13.16 million, with foreign guests accounting for 3.79 million. This pales in comparison with 2017's total of 53.6 million visitors, 7.4 million of whom were from overseas.

The fact that Kyoto has more Michelin-starred restaurants per capita than Paris attests to its status as a gourmet capital. As of 2020, Kyoto had 105 Michelin-starred establishments—one for roughly every 13,900 Kyotoites—whereas, Paris, with a population of over 11 million, had 119 venues with the coveted stars—one for roughly (only!) every 92,580 Parisians. Although France continues to hold onto its title as the country with the highest number of Michelin-starred restaurants, Japan claims top spot as the country with the highest density of them in the world.

Kyoto most likely has been awarded so many stars because its local cuisine has been built on a robust culture of high-quality and innovative culinary art stretching back over the centuries, typified by *cha-kaiseki* (banquet-style multi-course meals with roots in the traditional tea ceremony) and Shojin *ryori* (the vegetarian cuisine of Buddhist monks).

Although Michelin-starred restaurants in Kyoto include some specializing in Western cookery, most offer Japanese fare—mostly Kyoto cuisine, generically referred to as Kyo *ryori*. In this piece, I will be dealing specifically with Shojin *ryori* as I feel that this style of cooking is the most in harmony with nature.

*What Is Shojin* Ryori?
Shojin *ryori* developed along with Buddhism and its practices which came to Japan in the 6th century from India and China. The Buddhist vegetarian diet naturally came into being in keeping with the belief of *ahimsa* (compassion) or the principle of non-violence and respect for all living things. By consuming a diet free of animal flesh, Buddhist devotees were abstaining from violence against living things and thanking nature for its blessings and the bounty of the land. When Zen Buddhism started to spread across Japan in the Kamakura period (1185 to 1333), this vegetarian diet evolved into Shojin *ryori*. As Zen Buddhism gained momentum, Shojin *ryori* was continuously refined and perfected by Buddhist monks as part of their spiritual practice as "devotional dishes" to move forward on their path to enlightenment.

In Buddhism, the number five holds great significance. It can refer to the Five Strengths of faith, energy, mindfulness, concentration, and wisdom, in addition to other important philosophies and precepts. This number also has its place in Shojin *ryori*. When cooking, Buddhist monks used the "rule of five" so that meals were offered in five colors (green, yellow, red, black, and white) to complement the five flavors—sweet, sour, salty, bitter, and savory (*umami*). Five different methods were also applied in food preparation—stewing, boiling, roasting, steaming or just plain raw. These approaches were imaginatively combined to draw out the essential goodness and qualities of vegetable ingredients and create food that appealed to our five faculties. All this is achieved without the need to introduce additional flavorings in most cases. The culinary skills of Shojin chefs in Kyoto can sometimes be put to the test by the abundant choices of vegetables that are available throughout the year. Currently, 43 types of vegetables are certified as 京野菜 or *kyo-yasai*, Kyoto vegetables, 20 of which are designated as ブランド京野菜 or *burando kyo-yasai*, Kyoto brand vegetables. Moreover, the selection of dishes the chefs create must convey 季節感, or culinary aesthetic, that best expresses the season.

A crucial point in Shojin cuisine is that meals are prepared with care and mindfulness to use everything and waste nothing. This principle is fundamental to the cuisine and its origins. For example, vegetable peels and scraps can be recycled into stocks and pickles. Also, leftover boiled *konbu* seaweed used to make the essential *dashi* condiment can be simply cooked down with *shoyu* and *saké* to make *tsukudani*, which is an ideal companion side dish for plain boiled rice.

It's quite comforting to think that a culinary art form developed several centuries ago still has immediate relevance in this day and age. Countries around the world are advocating and advancing zero food loss and waste. Shojin *ryori* fits in perfectly with efforts like these to achieve an eco-friendly and resource-recycling society.

*Kajitsu—A Culinary Oasis*
Here, I would like to introduce an authentic Shojin *ryori* restaurant—嘉日, or Kajitsu, meaning good or auspicious day. This restaurant was conceived in Kyoto and entered this world not in the tranquil cradle of a 路地 *roji*, or secluded alleyway just off Gion, but in the hustle and bustle of New York City.

Kajitsu came to be in the mind of Shuichiro Kobori. He had dined in so-called Japanese restaurants in New York only to be dismayed and appalled at how Japanese culture had been misinterpreted and abused. "I felt as if something pure and pristine had been bastardized, violated and watered down until it had become barely recognizable," he writes in the commemorative publication *Kajitsu—A Shojin Restaurant's Season in the City*. He says, "This [Buddhist] notion of impermanence (無常 *mujo*), that everything has its season, nothing in this world is eternal, is foundational. What made me want to open Kajitsu in New York City, from the first, was my urge to share the truth of Japanese culture with the world. That said, how could the restaurant not, in itself, exemplify this philosophy."

Kajitsu opened and started serving Shojin cuisine in 2009 on the premise that it would close its doors several years down the line, no matter what.

To make Kobori's dream of presenting authentic Japanese culture in New York a reality, everything about the restaurant—its design, dining tables and counter, furniture and fittings, ceramic and lacquer tableware and serving vessels, vases, calligraphy, and even its earthen walls—had to be absolutely authentic. Kobori commissioned renowned 7th-generation Nara ceramic artist Shiro Tsujimura to create a selection of pieces exclusively for the restaurant. He also tasked a traditional carpenter—Keisuke Shimizu, based in Kyoto's neighboring Shiga Prefecture—to design and construct Kajitsu's interior in the form of the *sukiya* wooden building style dating from the Azuchi-Momoyama period (roughly 1573 to 1603). For this, Shimizu brought original lumber, such as 神代欅 or Jindai *keyaki* zelkova wood that had been laid beneath soil supposedly for centuries, all the way from Japan.

Any Japanese restaurant, of course, could not survive without talented and skilled chefs. Kobori recruited young but experienced chefs who had already established a name for themselves. Two of them had honed their culinary skills at Michelin-starred restaurants in Kyoto and Kanazawa. Although not all of Kyoto's indigenous vegetables could be procured in New York, these chefs applied their dexterity and art to make the best of available ingredients and produce dishes that would delight the palates of discerning New Yorkers in search of the authentic.

The seasons play a pivotal role in Japanese cuisine. The following passage from *Kajitsu—A Shojin Restaurant's Season in the City* sums this up well:

> *"The most important distinction between the way cuisine is conceived of in the East and in the West concerns the calendar and the seasons. The focus in Shojin cuisine isn't simply on what is 'in season,' but that which reflects upon the season past, and anticipates what is to come. A single meal pays respects to these aspects of seasonality in a multilayered, multifaceted way, and it is this regard for the blessings of the season that characterizes preparation and service in Shojin dining."*

Kobori's clarity of vision and determination to present Japanese culture in a pure light through the most traditional of Japanese cuisines paid off. Word of this new Japanese restaurant soon spread and made a big impression on New York's culinary landscape. Among its visitors were judges from the Michelin Guide who were so impressed that they awarded Kajitsu not one but two stars in its first year.

As planned, Kajitsu served its last meal on September 19, 2022. When I interviewed Kobori in January, I said that a lot of people felt that it was a shame to close while the restaurant was enjoying such success. "Not at all," he said. "I set out to present Japanese culture in an unadulterated form to New Yorkers. And, I achieved that. I have no regrets at all." As he wrote in his book, "I'm absolutely certain that the seeds of culture we've planted here will continue to grow

10, 20, 100 years into the future, and will still be producing enormous flowers."

I certainly hope so.

*Afterthought*
As I sit here putting the finishing touches to this piece, I know for a fact that *na-no-hana* (rape blossoms) should be on sale round about now at the Masukata 商店街 *shotengai*, my favorite shopping arcade near Demachi-yanagi Station. *Na-no-hana* will most likely be followed by *karashina* mustard greens, *fuki-no-to* edible Petasites japonicus buds, *tara-no-me* Fatsia sprouts and other *sansai* wild vegetable delicacies in February and March. I know this instinctively. Live a few years in Kyoto and the sense of the seasons will become part of your DNA. You will come to anticipate and relish seasonal vegetables as they become available. Here, nature and time progress, but there is little sensation of change or movement; seasons flow seamlessly into each other to offer the blessings of nature for all to enjoy. I have grown accustomed to and comfortable in the thought that things this year will be the same always and in coming years, too—this is Kyoto's soft predictability.

*Acknowledgement*
I would like to thank Shuichiro Kobori for allowing me to interview him and quote from his *Kajitsu—A Shojin Restaurant's Season in the City*. The book also provides lots of seasonal recipes for Shojin cuisine dishes, and describes cooking essentials such as how to prepare various *dashi* stock, which is an all important, vital element of Japanese cooking. It is available on amazon.com. Kobori's company's website can be found at www.fuka-kyoto.jp.

❋

**Julian Holmes** earned his B.A. (Hons) in Japanese at London University and came to Japan initially for two years. He is currently in his 43rd year here, 33 of which have been in Kyoto, and believes moving to Japan was one of the best decisions of his life. He has been a professional translator for the past 38 years and is currently working on his first book, *Moss Garden—David Bowie's Love Affair With Kyoto*. He loves fine wine, fusion and jazz, and has a very soft spot for his adorable grandchildren.

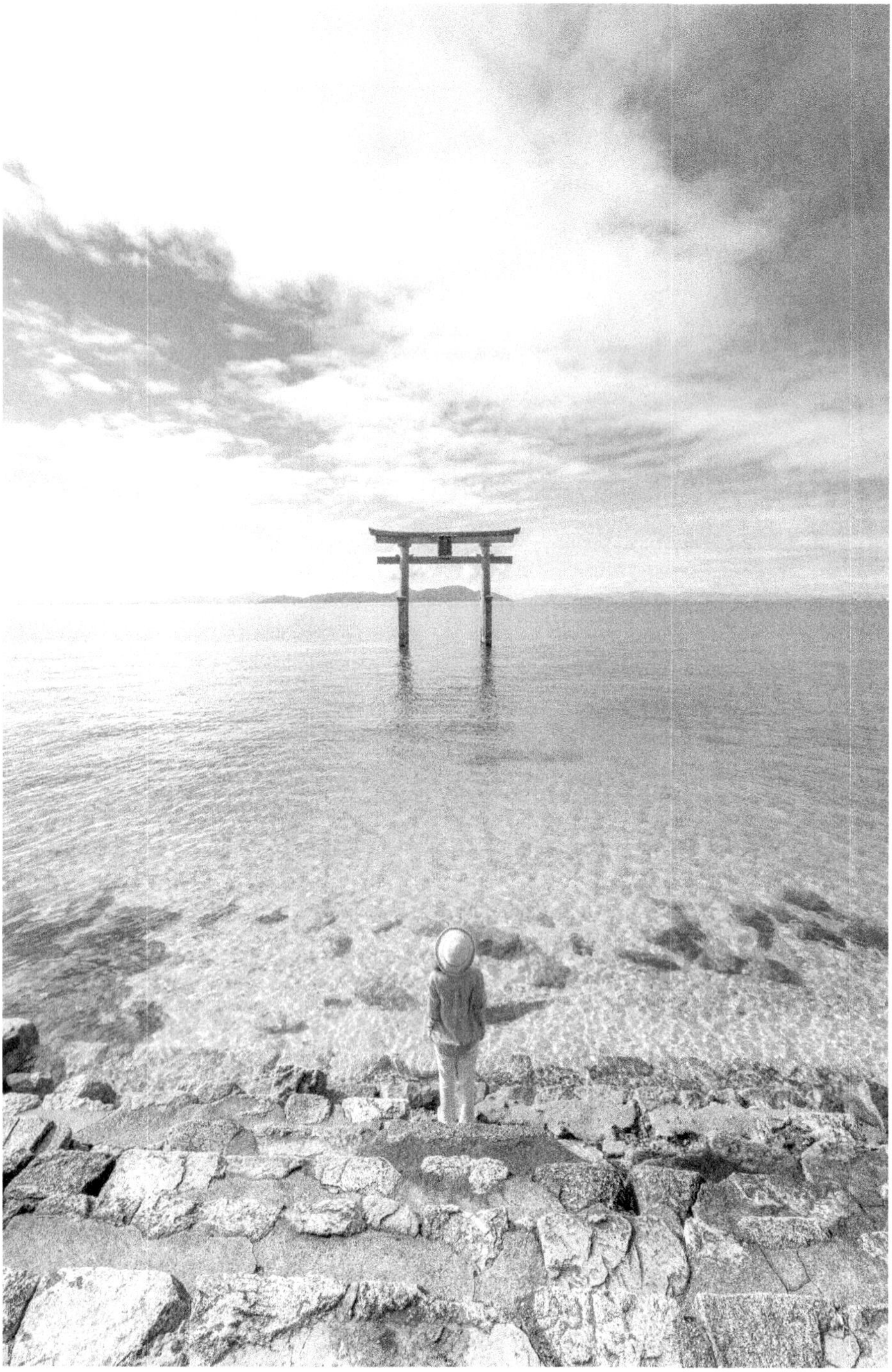

# Recollections of Nature, Neighbors, and Nibbles

KAREN LEE TAWARAYAMA

My mother was raised in Brooklyn, New York, but spent her summers among the forests and lakes of Girl Scout camps in northern New York State. She always wished that I would grow up to be a "nature girl"—one who has an appreciation for immersing myself in the peaceful outdoors. She must have been very happy that in 1999, my ALT placement was in a rural town in Kyoto's neighboring Shiga Prefecture, minutes from Japan's largest lake. Lake Biwa, seemingly as vast as a small ocean, is like a calm sheet of glass which reflects the sky's changing hues. Beyond fields of rice and pine tree-dotted shores, a misty expanse of white sometimes appears as a meeting of heaven and earth. My hometown had rolling farmland and a lake located minutes away, so such scenery provided comfort and familiarity. My husband's work duties eventually brought us one hour south to Kyoto city, which has now become my permanent home.

*

We settled into a residential neighborhood in the north of the city which provided a serene locale and abundance of nature. The main thoroughfare was known for its fashionable shops and cafés, but the residential streets retained much of the flavor of the Japanese countryside, as the subway had only been extended this far in October 1990. Many streets had towering clusters of sunflowers and were lined with vegetable patches and greenhouses containing plump tomatoes, cucumbers, and eggplants; my husband and I referred to one particular street leading to the subway station as

"Farm Street." Narrow waterways flowed closer to the mountains, and short, narrow stone bridges allowed access to homes.

I got much of my nature fix in the nearby Kyoto Botanical Gardens. The grounds of approximately 240,000 square meters provided time for quiet contemplation and relaxation. We enjoyed tulips, irises, peonies, azaleas, and hydrangeas in the spring. Summer brought lotuses and the opportunity for moon viewing. In autumn we walked among numerous varieties of fragrant roses, cascading multi-colored Japanese maple leaves, and the culturally symbolic chrysanthemum. Finally, winter brought the delight of blooming white, purple, and pink orchids. Throughout the year we enjoyed strolling beneath an overarching canopy of ninety-two century-old *kusunoki* (camphor) trees; their tamed and miniature neighbors in the *bonsai* garden induced awe. We also had a glimpse into the lifestyles of Japan's senior citizens. With free access, many were out and about in all seasons with backpacks, cameras, and easels.

To the immediate west, the banks of the Kamo River offered mountain views, trees to sit beneath, walking paths to enjoy, benches for lounging, maintained lawns for picnics on comfortable days, and serenely waving grasses. To the north of our residence was the small and rustic Oota Shrine, a subsidiary of nearby Kamigamo Shrine, a World Heritage Site. Oota Shrine, nestled within a serene forest and framed by a field of purple irises in mid-May, provided calm. Directly beside the shrine was Oota Komichi, a narrow road leading to a well-hidden residential street and connected to a very narrow dirt path snaking further up the mountain.

*

Opposite our apartment was a small Japanese pickle shop. The owner, Mitsui-san, stood on the corner as children walked to the adjacent elementary school, guiding them as many older adults do throughout the city. Mitsui-san had resided in this neighborhood for many decades. I was curious about the mountain path, and one day I decided to pick his brain for more information.

"*Sono michi wa zettai ni hitori de ikande!* Never walk up that path by yourself!" he warned me in Kansai dialect.

While Oota Komichi may have been well-trodden at one point in time, he noted that I should take caution because it was now the habitat of many *inoshishi* (wild boars), *tanuki* (raccoons), *shika* (deer), and *saru* (monkeys).

Mitsui-san believed that it took a village to raise a child and often lamented to me, a young mother, that parents were not as strict with their children as they used to be. The presence of adults with a balance of gentleness and firmness developed strong character, he explained. As I approached our home with my infant son and we saw Mitsui-san on the corner, he would push his spectacles up his nose and give my child a toothy grin, punctuating the final syllable of his repeated greeting, "*KonnichiWA! KonnichiWA!*" Local residents would drop into Mitsui-san's store to extend greetings and to purchase pickled *suguki*, a local specialty made from a hybrid of *daikon* (winter radish) and *kabu* (Japanese turnip). The front room of his shop had a desk, benches, refrigerated containers, and large wooden display barrels with plastic pickle packages laid just so.

As Mitsui-san was a neighborhood fixture, he was perfectly suited to make connections. One day he approached me saying, "Karen-san, you're an English conversation teacher. Someone living on the next street is interested in speaking with you." At that time I was meeting privately with students here and there, at homes and at cafés. I welcomed more work and found pleasure in meeting new people. In the coming week I rang the doorbell of a tall, narrow, three-story home and was greeted at the gate by a smiling man with a thick mop of gray hair. Thus began a friendship with my gentle neighbor, Yasuda-san.

After entering the sliding front door and slipping off my shoes at the *genkan* (entryway), Yasuda-san directed me to a compact room on the southern end of the first floor with a small, raised area of rush-covered straw *tatami* mats in the corner and a coffee table and sofa situated on the carpeted area before it. We met here almost every

Saturday morning for the next two years to have hour-long conversations. Yasuda-san always sat with perfect posture and treated each lesson with more reverence than I personally thought necessary for obvious reviews of his knowledge. He told me that our conversations helped to keep his mind active, in addition to being a lovely time to share our cultures.

Yasuda-san's residence was the only house I had ever known to have its own elevator. His wife would descend from the second-floor kitchen toward the end of our lessons each week carrying a small, decorative tray with a specially prepared item—a new adventure for the taste buds. As time went on, it seemed that Yasuda-san was more excited about the inevitable treats than the lesson itself. The sweets were most often from Kyoto-based companies. I could sense Yasuda-san's great pride in his city, although his words and attitude were never boastful. He was simply a connoisseur of traditional confectioneries. Was the point of our lessons really to practice English conversation, or his generous cultural sharing?

Yasuda-san explained that he had always had a sweet tooth, an appetite for special finds, and felt intrigued by the ways of foreign people. Like Mitsui-san, Yasuda-san had also been raised in this neighborhood and shared with me his own early memories of the area. For example, the Kyoto Botanical Gardens had opened in 1924, but were used by occupying US Forces as residential grounds after the end of World War II. I was surprised to learn from him that the local citizens were prohibited from entering the gardens until restoration in 1961. Yasuda-san recalled that during the Occupation, he was not permitted to study English at school. However, he and his friends would venture to the gates where they hoped to encounter residents. "Please," Yasuda-san said he would ask them, with an eager hand extended. "Please, give me chocolate."

*

"Please taste this," Yasuda-san's wife said gently, placing a small dish before me on the coffee table. These treasured opportunities helped me develop an appreciation for the imagery of Kyoto's nature expressed in traditional sweets. I have the distinct memory of partaking in a summer edition of five *dorayaki* (two castella patties with red bean filling) from the confectionary maker Sasaya Iori, which was originally established in Kyoto in 1716. Each *dorayaki* was printed with the characters of the Gozan Okuribi—fires lit yearly on Kyoto's surrounding mountains in August, meant to guide visiting ancestors home to the spirit world at the close of the Obon Festival. The Japanese mindset connects deeply with seasonal flow, and it is delightful to confirm this connection through snacks and confectioneries shared with friends and loved ones. In autumn, Yasuda-san and I munched on rice crackers which had been packaged in a thick paper of deep red, adorned with gold-trimmed orange and yellow leaves. At the height of Kyoto's summer humidity, our plates had cubes of pale aquamarine blue, meant to visually evoke a cool sensation.

\*

After I had known Yasuda-san for several months, my mother happened to travel from the United States to Kyoto and was warmly welcomed to join me at his home. They were practically the same age and took much time to speak about their respective childhoods and how they had envisioned each other's countries and cultures in times of war and peace. In accordance with Yasuda-san's regular exquisite show of *omotenashi* (hospitality), that day he and his wife seemed even more determined to prepare something special.

"This is *yakimochi* from Jinbado, a shop just beside Kamigamo Shrine," Yasuda-san explained as he set a dish of grilled rice cakes filled with sweet *azuki* (red bean) paste before my mother. My husband and I were familiar with the shop, which opens at 7:00 am and consistently sells all products within the morning; one must arrive early to be guaranteed a box. Yasuda-san had gone there right after he woke up, determined that my mother should have a taste. Yasuda-san's wife brought into the room powdered *matcha*, made from tea leaves harvested in Kyoto's Uji district, and proceeded to whisk the powder before our eyes with her bamboo *chasen* into a luxurious froth. It was my mother's first taste of freshly prepared green tea, and she closed her eyes while placing her lips on their earthen Raku tea bowl to take a sip.

\*

Time marches on, and more than ten years have passed since my family moved further down the river. In August 2022 I had the opportunity to make an impromptu visit to the pickle shop. Mitsui-san and his wife were chatting in the front room with two relatives and welcomed me in for relief from the intense afternoon heat. The strong sunlight that year had been particularly detrimental to the *suguki*, they sighed. The farmers had little luck with their harvest, so there were hardly enough to prepare a sufficient number of pickles. I walked down Farm Street after our conversation and was, indeed, surprised to observe several greenhouses which seemed to have small, wilted, and abandoned eggplants. I felt a pang of sadness and wondered how other vegetables had fared, and also if such hardship would follow in the coming years due to the increased warming of our planet.

Some things never change, however. Long after I had moved to another neighborhood and had taken up my current university position, I was surprised to see an incoming call from Yasuda-san on my smartphone screen.

"*Moshi moshi*," I answered expectantly.

"*Moshi moshi*. Ah, Karen-san! *Gobusata shite imasu* (It has been a while)!" Yasuda-san responded in a voice shakier, but just as exuberant. "I'm with a group of walking friends. You'll never guess where I am!" he continued in Japanese. My mind conjured an image of their group in brimmed hats and carrying small backpacks. "I'm sure you can't get away from the office right now, but we're at a café near your campus, enjoying delicious ice cream sodas! It made me think of you."

I was delighted to know that, despite the passing years, Yasuda-san had never lost his sweet tooth. It also never hurts to be associated with "sweet." My heart was happy.

※

**Karen Lee Tawarayama** was raised in beautiful Bucks County, Pennsylvania (USA). She lived in India, Kenya, and the Middle East before settling in Japan. Her professional work involves the internationalization of a centuries-old Buddhist university, and her freelance narrations and voiceovers can be heard throughout Japan, including at the Osaka Castle Museum, Yoyogi National Stadium, and Narita International Airport. She organizes the annual Writers in Kyoto Writing Competition and was Co-Editor of *Structures of Kyoto* (WiK Anthology 4). As a hobby, she enjoys interviewing local people and uploading their stories to her blog, *Kyoto Faces*.

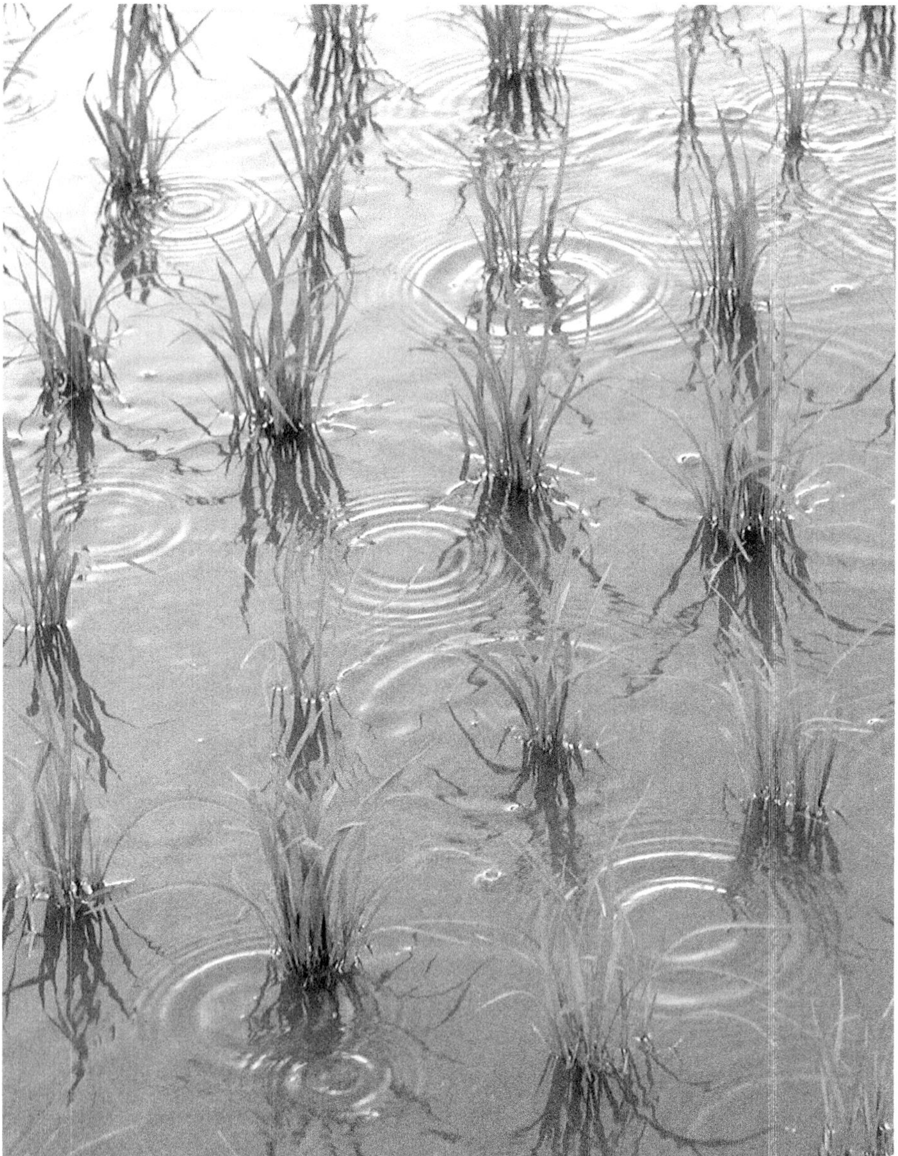

# Local News

KEN RODGERS

Newly retired, at age 70, I've quit browsing Google news. Barefoot in warm mud, hand-weeding our water-filled rice field in the mostly unpeopled Sakahara valley, northern Iwakura, I've drifted into a new, less filtered way of connecting with what's happening in the world: simply listening.

By tuning my consciousness into the so-called void, I'm getting local news directly from the open-source calls of cranes and ever-vigilant kites (*tombi*) overhead, wingbeats of wild ducks in rapid transit, the pronouncements of an out-of-season *uguisu* up in the hillside forest, the ebulliently ubiquitous buzz-sawing of fat brown *abura-semi* cicadas, random conversations among off-the-grid communities of frogs, the disputative caucuses of crows, the haunting late-afternoon refrain of a *higurashi* cicada, occasional shared soliloquies of crickets, the gentle trickling of irrigation channels, the constant undertone of the mid-valley stream setting out on its journey to the sea, the sometimes swelling patter of raindrops, occasional pure silences.

Aside from these timeless emanations from non-human sources, I may hear whispering high-altitude intrusions of planet-circling airliners, the roar of neighboring farmers' weed-whackers, tireless *taiko* drumming at a nearby alternative school, or quiet songs voiced by a local woman who sometimes walks through the valley for exercise or simply time out…

For me, listening has become a way of focusing outwards, beyond self: switching off an internal monologue of recycled media-bytes, revisited fixations of memory and closed-circuit mental meanderings—all essentially irrelevant to the bigger picture, the vast real-time natural soundscape of an actual day in progress.

As I see it now, conventional meditative practice, sitting Buddha-style, deliberately maintaining existential awareness of in-breath and out-breath—while useful as a centering mindfulness technique—may in fact be counter-effective. Anchoring consciousness to one's own physical body seems virtually guaranteed to result in a self-centered perception of existence. By merely listening intently, near to far, while engaged in physical work, I briefly free myself from the mind-babble of my illusory self.

The precisely in-the-present moment that I tune into, or align awareness with, is also indivisibly the eternal—that ongoing flow and constant graceful dance of the cosmos which has—at least from a human perspective—no beginning and no ending. I'm hearing each installment of local news in Sakahara's vast audiobook of the infinite in the same instant that it is being recorded.

Gradually, I'm finding it easier to maintain that momentary focus, despite distractions inherent to everyday tasks at hand in attending to the perceived needs of rice and vegetables.

I recall words that I first encountered over fifty years ago, in Paul Reps' *Zen Flesh, Zen Bones*:

"Toss attachments for body aside, realizing I am everywhere. One who is everywhere is joyous."

The short-lived mid-summer cicadas know this, for sure. They speak of nothing else, incessantly.

❃

**Ken Rodgers**, originally from Tasmania, has resided in semi-rural Iwakura for over thirty years. He is one of the founders of *Kyoto Journal*; managing editor since 1992. He is currently compiling a new not-for-publication prose/poetry/photos collection, provisionally titled *Another Eon Slips By*.

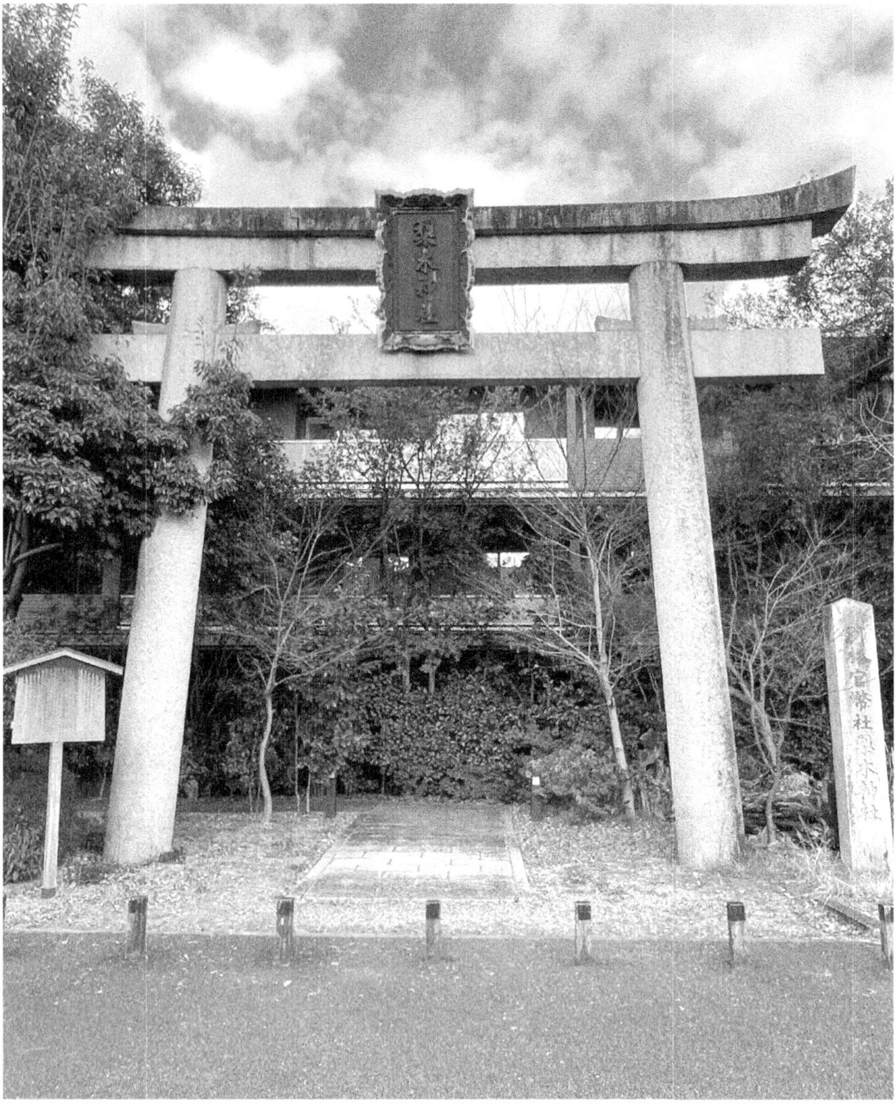

# Nashinoki Shrine makes Lifestyle Changes

KIRSTY KAWANO

Just over the eastern wall of Kyoto's Imperial Palace is a pretty little shrine that is making changes.

When you stand before the tall, stone *torii* gate of Nashinoki Shrine, you may be disappointed by what you see in front of you, or you may be fascinated. Either way, take the path below the *torii*. Follow it to the dead end a few meters ahead and then turn left. Continue until you come to the gravel road and look to your right to see the sign that shows you where to go next. The sign marks the continuation of the path and an entrance that is almost a tunnel formed by the fine, outstretched branches of the *hagi*, the Japanese bush clover. When the path turns again, this time to the left, those who were disappointed will see what they had been expecting: still far off in the distance are the shrine's main buildings.

What was this detour about? Survival.

Nashinoki is one of Kyoto's "newer" shrines. It was founded in 1885, well after the national capital had moved to Tokyo. It is dedicated to court noble Sanetsumu Sanjo and his son Sanetomi as deities of learning and literature, and for their services and loyalty to the imperial house and the restoration of its rule. It is situated on a long sliver of land between the Imperial Palace and Teramachi Street.

As well as the shrine buildings and the 500 *hagi* bushes that line the pathways, the shrine is also home to the last of Kyoto's three famed natural water springs. There is no charge to enter the shrine grounds. Like most of Kyoto City's 300 or so shrines, its income is limited to sales of amulets and fortune slips, prayer and wedding service fees and its *saisen* box that gathers monetary offerings for the gods. While these funds may be sufficient to cover daily management costs, they fall short of the sum needed to cover the *shikinen senguu* reconstruction of key shrine buildings that occurs once every few decades. Shrines look to donations to raise such funds. But for Nashinoki, a lesser-known shrine with no parishioners, that was a struggle, so it came up with a different idea to fund the restoration of its 130-year-old main building. Between the first and second of its tall, concrete *torii* gates is a three-storey apartment building.

Eagle Court at the Kyoto Imperial Palace, Nashinoki Shrine, was built in 2015 on a 60-year land lease. The rent from the development has provided the shrine with a stable income. The building is a bland, dark hue, hidden on three sides behind a layer of foliage. Despite its discreet appearance, the Association of Shinto Shrines would not approve the development plan, so Nashinoki left the organization. It is not the only shrine facing difficulty maintaining its presence in Kyoto City. In 2012, citing financial difficulties, Shusse Inari Shrine sold the land that it had occupied for more than 400 years in Kamigyo Ward and moved to Ohara in the northern outskirts of the city. An apartment building was built in its place.

Even famous shrines are struggling. The UNESCO World Heritage-listed Shimogamo Shrine in 2017 constructed eight 3-storey buildings with a total of 107 apartments on a section of its land at the opposite end from its main shrine. The 50-year land lease is said to have raised 1 billion yen, which, together with annual land rent of 80 million yen, helped fund the 2015 *shikinen senguu* that was believed to have cost 3 billion yen. The development replaced a car park and training hall. The shrine has said it plans to take the land back and demolish the apartment buildings when the lease expires.

In realigning itself for the future, Nashinoki Shrine has not stopped at its real estate deal. A set of rental bicycles is located on the premises, and in July 2022, a coffee stand opened in its courtyard. It uses water from the shrine's famous Somei Well for its specialty cold-brew coffee.

In September, when the *hagi* blooms, Nashinoki Shrine holds its annual festival. Visitors come to see displays of archery, the tea ceremony, Kyogen plays and traditional dance and music, and to tie their original *waka* poems to the *hagi* branches. Helping to ensure the future of such leisures of the past is the lifestyle of the present. The nature of a city with a long and rich history is that it knows time is always moving forward, and that we must move with it.

※

**Kirsty Kawano** is a translator and editor who mainly writes non-fiction for free-to-read online publications. She has lived long-term in Kyoto, Tokyo and her hometown of Melbourne, Australia.

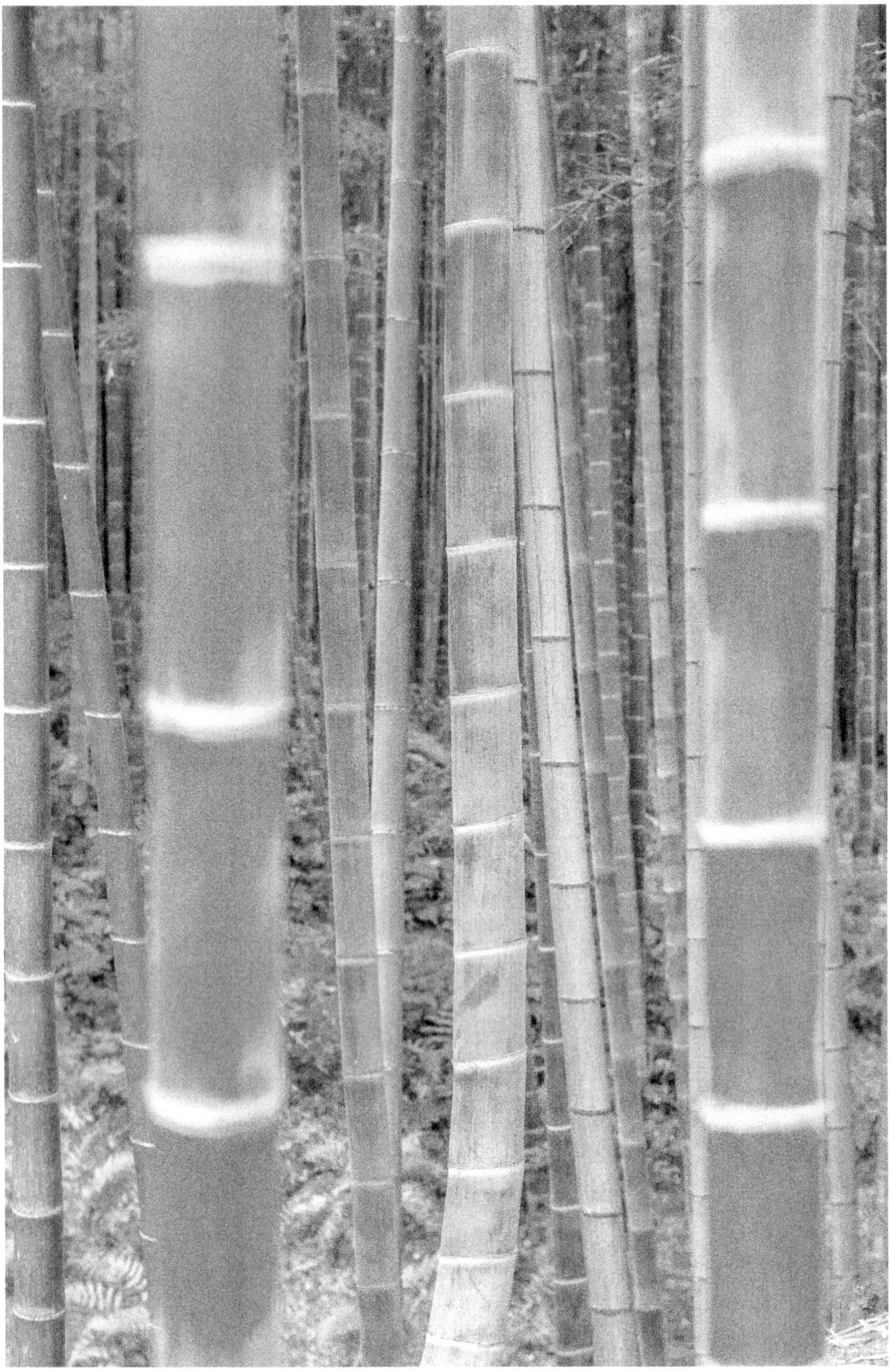

# Summer Rain

LISA TWARONITE SONE

"Who's this beautiful lady, Obaa-chan?"

My daughter Anna pointed to an image in the velvet-covered album. Most of the sepia people had passed away long ago.

It was afternoon, but Anna was still wearing her nightgown. She'd said it was too hot to get dressed, and we weren't going anywhere in the rain, anyway. Now she was stretched out on the tatami, a wraith-like billow of white cotton, with the family albums spread around her.

My in-laws' home in Kyoto didn't have any of the latest electronic toys, but its dusty closets were full of treasures for visiting grandchildren to discover: old photos, glass marbles, wooden tops and scraps of colorful silk. The house was a traditional *machiya* built right next the street, whose modest facade belied the depth of its rooms and garden. The muffled patter of the rainfall outside could be mistaken for the voices of people whispering behind the house's paper screens.

On gloomy summer days like this one, when the mist from the downpour mingled with the stifling humidity, the concepts of past, present and future can become fluid and almost interchangeable. All cities are built upon the bones and the dust of countless people who came before us, but the pulse of human history beats much closer to the surface in Kyoto. Lines often blur between light and shadow, the natural and the supernatural, the living and the dead.

"That's me!" my mother-in-law told her. Obaa-chan was sipping tea under the *kotatsu*, whose heater was switched off in the summer. It was covered with a thin tablecloth to hide the earthen pit where the smoldering charcoal used to be placed, in the years before electricity.

Obaa-chan had a fuzzy beige shawl wrapped around her shoulders to protect herself from the blast of the air conditioner she'd turned on for the sake of her visitors, though the old unit barely stirred the air of the cavernous room. "That was my *omiai* photo," she told Anna. "The matchmaker who arranged my marriage showed it to your grandfather, and he wanted to meet me."

Anna had resumed flipping through the album. "Is this your family, Obaa-chan? Your big sister was beautiful, too."

Obaa-chan set down her cup and picked up her magnifying glass to examine the photo Anna placed before her, of a couple and their six children: one son and five daughters, all dressed in formal *kimono*, none of them smiling.

Obaa-chan was the smallest. She looked a bit younger than Anna was now, maybe around five or six, and yet I understood why my daughter had immediately recognized her. The little girl in the photo remarkably resembled the white-haired woman Obaa-chan had become: the same wide nose and high forehead, her mouth pursed in the same expression of determination as she looked directly at the camera.

She was leaning against a lovely older girl whose gaze shifted upward, as if she were looking for something in the sky.

"Yes, my Nee-chan was so beautiful," Obaa-chan sighed. "She was my favorite sister, like a second mother to me. This photo was the last time we were all together."

"Do you still meet her?" Anna asked.

I already knew the answer. My husband had cautioned me never to ask Obaa-chan about her sister, so I hoped Anna's questions wouldn't bring up any painful memories.

Like the city of Kyoto, Obaa-chan's rural hometown in the mountains had survived the second World War physically unscathed by bombs but far from intact, as many of its sons and daughters departed and never returned. Obaa-chan's beloved teenage sister was forced to leave home to work in a munitions factory, where she contracted tuberculosis and died.

I was therefore surprised when Obaa-chan told Anna, "Yes, sometimes I do."

"So she's still alive?"

"She is to me, and I'm alive, so doesn't that make her alive, too? Aren't the people in your dreams sometimes real?"

Anna frowned as she considered this.

Obaa-chan asked her, "Do you want to hear a ghost story?"

Anna nodded and tucked her feet under the *kotatsu* next to her grandmother.

Obaa-chan took a long sip of her tea before she continued, "One night, when I was a girl around your age, I was sleeping, when I heard my Nee-chan outside calling my name. 'Junko! Junko!' I thought it was a dream, but I heard it again. 'Junkooooooo!'

"I was the only one in my family who heard it. No one else woke up. It was so dark and cold—I don't know why I wasn't afraid. I went downstairs and unlocked the door, and looked out. And can you guess what I saw?"

Anna shook her head.

"It was my Nee-chan, returning home! She had gone to work in Osaka. All the men were drafted to fight in the war, so the big girls who weren't married yet had to take the men's places to keep the factories running.

"At first, Nee-chan sent us letters, saying she missed us but the food was good and she had made many friends. But then one spring night, the Americans dropped the first firebombs. Fortunately, Nee-chan was living near a river and knew how to swim, so she could escape from the flames. The bombs stopped for a few months, but Nee-chan got sick…very sick. She'd been hiding in the cold river water for too long, and she was weak and thin. She'd probably lied to us about having enough to eat. It wasn't only pneumonia—she also had TB. We got a telegram saying she'd been admitted to a hospital. There weren't any nurses, so our mother had to go take care of her.

"Then in June, we heard that the bombing had started again. Bombs fell on Osaka through August, right up until the final day of the war. Back then, homes didn't have telephones, and mail rarely came, so my family had no idea if our mother and Nee-chan had survived. My mother later told us she heard the Emperor's speech on the radio….but she couldn't bear to tell Nee-chan the news of the surrender. So instead she told her Japan had won!

"Nee-chan must have known she was dying, and my mother didn't want her to believe she was giving her life to a lost cause. She passed away a few days later, thinking her sacrifice had helped Japan's victory."

Here Obaa-chan sighed, and then turned to me. She looked into my eyes, as directly as she had stared into the camera in the old family portrait.

"My mother's lie about the war used to bother me. But when I had children of my own, I understood why she told it. She wanted Nee-chan to think her brief life had a purpose. And of course she also didn't want to believe she'd lost her daughter for nothing."

I had no words to respond to this, to the loss of a child—the rarely spoken but always-present fear of every parent. I looked down at my own daughter wiping the sweat away from her eyes with the hem of her nightgown. Outside, the rain dripped off the eaves onto the garden stones, marking a wet rhythm of time like a clock ticking underwater.

Anna's voice interrupted the quiet. "So you saw Nee-chan's ghost outside the door that night?"

"No," Obaa-chan said. "I only heard her voice. I opened the door and there was a figure in a white mourning *kimono*. It looked just like a ghost, but it was my mother, holding Nee-chan's ashes in a box in front of her. She'd been calling my name to come unlock the door, but her voice had sounded just like Nee-chan's. I was so happy to see her! But I was also sad I would never meet my Nee-chan in person again, just in my dreams.

"My mother had no way to let us know Nee-chan had died. Telegram service had stopped. Everything was chaos, in those months after the surrender. One day—it must have been autumn because it was getting cold—my mother put on her mourning *kimono* and walked to a station, carrying Nee-chan's ashes. The train was full but she humbly begged to be allowed to board, to take her daughter's ashes home, and a kind man took pity on her and gave up his own seat for her. She took the train as far as she could, then walked for hours in the night to our village. Finally, here she was!"

Obaa-chan was finished. She turned her attention back to her teacup, swirling the green dregs inside.

Anna asked, "And then? What happened next?"

"We had a funeral for Nee-chan that week. We were lucky we had her ashes—there were lots of empty graves in those days, because so many people were gone without a trace."

"And then?"

"That's all. Life went on, the way it always does. I grew up and left my parents' village to marry your grandfather, and came to live in this house in Kyoto."

I could tell Anna had been hoping for a much more dramatic ending. "So this wasn't a real ghost story after all?"

This made Obaa-chan laugh. "Wasn't it? I heard my Nee-chan's voice, calling me."

"But you said it was your mother calling you. Didn't she say anything else to you?"

"We talked in the morning. That night, she was so exhausted she went right to sleep. All she said was my name, and *'Taidaima.'* I'm home."

Anna was disappointed. I knew it would be years before she fully appreciated what Obaa-chan had told her, so it was up to me to write it down for her so she remembered it all: the heat, the whispering rain, her grandmother shivering in her shawl under the air conditioner's feeble chill, and the photo albums spread across the *tatami*.

Someday, when the old house is gone and Anna only meets me and Obaa-chan in her dreams, she might tell her own family about her childhood summers in Kyoto, where the ghost stories are real— and about the final homecoming of her beautiful great-aunt who died young, believing Japan had won the war.

※

**Lisa Twaronite Sone** is a former journalist who now divides her time between Tokyo and Kyoto. Most of her short stories are fiction, but this one is true.

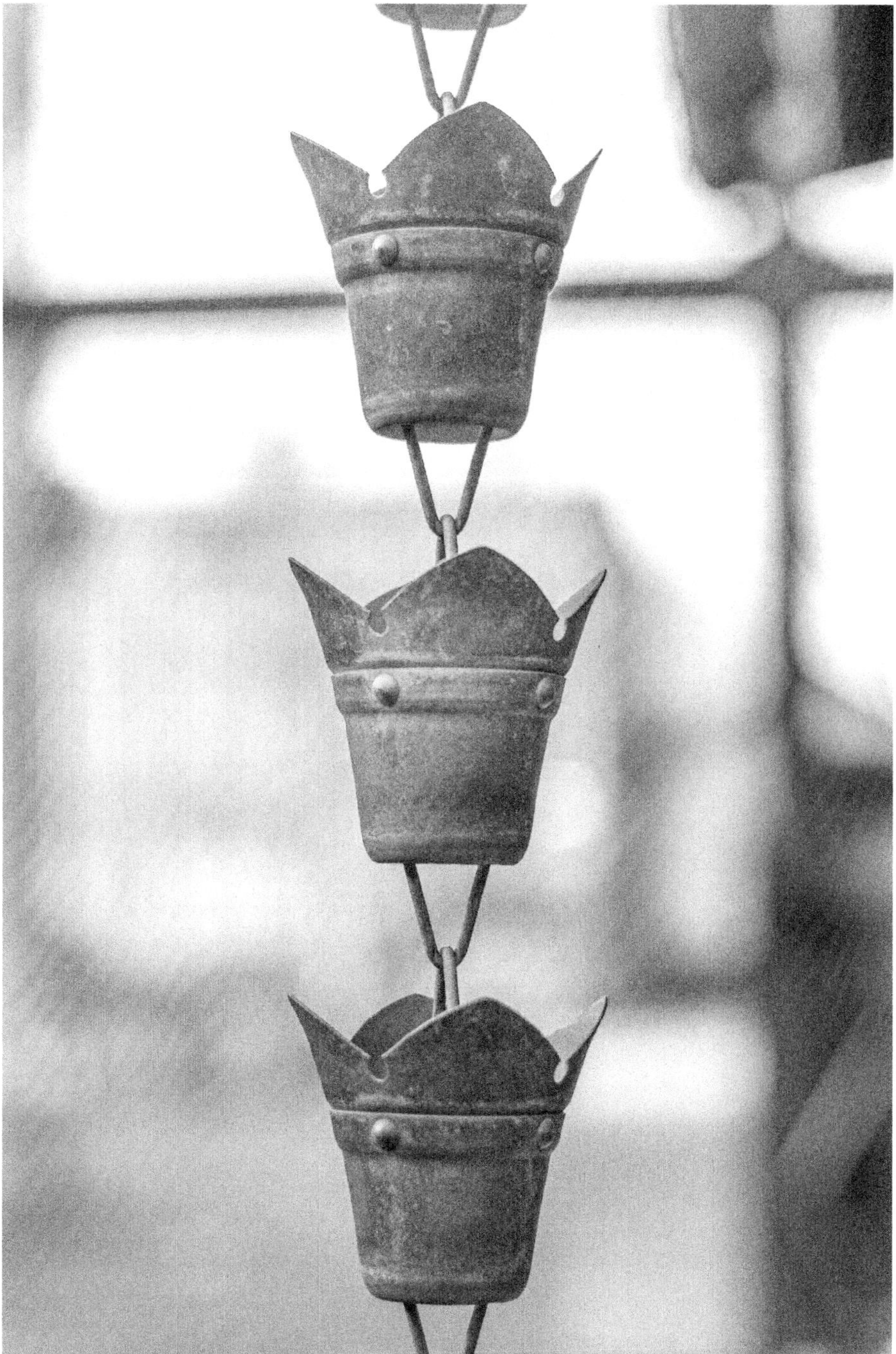

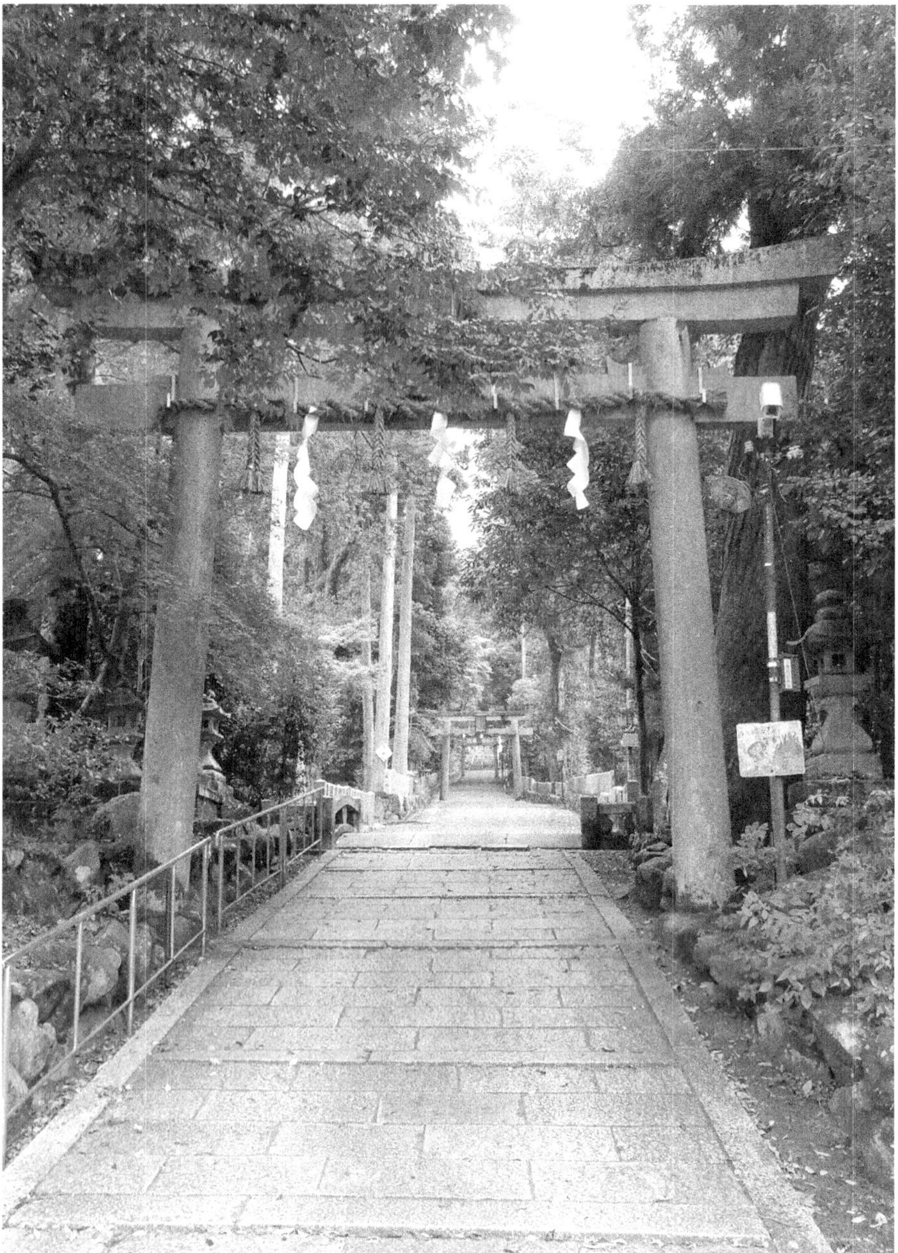

# Sudou Shrine

MALCOLM LEDGER

It is 5 a.m. on a Sunday, and we are on our way to the farmer's market in Ohara. The roads are empty and the great pine-clad mountains stand out with exceptional clarity in the early morning sunshine.

When we arrive, a few shoppers there before us are already picking carefully through the colourful vegetables, fruit, flowers, and herbs on display. We take our time, make our selections, and head home a short while later, content with our full shopping bags.

On the way back, the entrance to a Shinto shrine at the side of the road in Kami Takano catches our eye, and we decide to take a closer look.

It seems that the spirit of Prince Sawara Shinno (died 785 C.E.) is enshrined here. He was the younger brother of Emperor Kammu, who founded Kyoto in 794 C.E., and was therefore the Crown Prince.

In the fourth year of Emperor Kammu's reign (785 C.E.), he was apparently implicated in a plot to assassinate Fujiwara Tanefusa, a member of the powerful Fujiwara clan, and was arrested and confined at Otokuni temple. While on his way to exile on Awaji island, he protested his innocence by refusing to eat or drink, and consequently died. (The journey was long enough then that a man could starve himself to death.)

Several close relatives of Emperor Kammu then died in succession, and Kyoto was struck by a plague. These events were thought to be caused by Sawara Shinno's resentful ghost, and in order to appease it, the Imperial court awarded him the posthumous title of Emperor Sudou in 801 C.E. It built Sudou shrine exclusively for him, reburying him on Yajima.

This idea that natural disasters, plagues, and famine are caused by *onryo* (honourable spirits), who died with a grudge or in an unnatural way, is called Goryo Shinko, (the religion of ghosts), an offshoot belief of Shinto. Kyoto still boasts Kami Goryo and Shimo Goryo shrines, all built to appease various *onryo*, including Prince Sawara's.

Sudou Jinja itself is a large shrine, with a long, imposing gravel path leading up to rows of stone steps in the far distance. On either side are short concrete pillars inscribed with the names of its many supporters, and three large *torii* gateways span the path ahead. They are engraved on the back with the names of those who paid for them and the date of their erection.

The way is flanked by a cathedral of dark, towering *hinoki* pines. The early morning silence is broken only by birds, well-hidden, and flitting about somewhere overhead, and by the steady crunch of our footsteps on the gravel. We are the only visitors at this early hour.

The natural setting of Shinto shrines reminds us that our very survival depends on re-connecting, and re-linking with what so many still think of as 'other', but which is in fact our nourishing womb and the source of our very existence.

As with so many large shrines, Sudou Jinja is an oasis of peace, a place to escape from the noisy modern world, a place to reflect and take stock. It provides a respite, a balm to our souls. Here we can once again feel our deep connection with the surrounding natural world which nourishes and sustains us. Here we could even imagine hugging trees and talking to them, so close do we feel to them. And we can also consider how we have arrogantly usurped our role within the natural world, and how technology has enabled us to do it.

Over the hundreds of millions of years of life's existence on the planet, we can consider how we have come to place ourselves at its pinnacle, though no more than one species among countless, equally valuable, others. We can consider how greed and the pursuit of profit have ruined our minds and severed our bonds with what is holy and worthy of reverence. We can consider how it is we who, in the end, shall be crushed, humbled, and punished for our overweening arrogance, hubris, despoliation, and ruthless exploitation of the natural world, which does not belong to us. And we shall have deserved it.

For the ancient Japanese, Japan was the land of innumerable *kami*, spirits who inhabited every rock, tree, mountain and grove, and who co-existed peacefully with the human world. Monotheism and its accompanying theology were concepts which never occurred to them. It was the angry, resentful spirits of departed humans which were to be feared and placated, not a jealous God, and this idea later became the material for many Noh plays.

There we find animistic ghosts, ghosts of the dead, ghosts who possess others, and vengeful ghosts. They are not all to be feared, however, for some of them show the agony of death in battle, and the unrequited longing of love, as well as malevolent ghosts who attack the living.

In 1872, as Japan opened up to the world, the Meiji government forbad belief in ghosts, goblins, and all 'superstitious practices'. Mountains such as Mt. Fujii and Mt. Omine, which had previously been off-limits to women, now became accessible to them.

Belief in spirits is still very much alive in twenty-first century Japan, and can be found in festivals such as Obon in August, in which the spirits of the dead are thought to visit the living. They are welcomed with fires lit in front of houses, and Kyoto helps guide them back to their abodes in the spirit world by lighting bonfires on the surrounding mountains.

Further down the path, and to the right, is a bamboo pipe spouting water from the mountain into a round pool of moss-covered rocks. Those who wish to demonstrate their religious discipline may stand beneath the waterfall to pray, usually in the winter, wearing only a loin cloth or thin, white garment.

An information board says that an epitaph of Ono no Emishi is to be found higher up the mountain. He was a member of the Grand Council of State and Minister of Justice during the reign of Emperor Temmu (673–686 C.E.). Surprisingly, this epitaph has been designated as a national treasure, not necessarily because of who Ono no Emishi was, but perhaps because it is a relic of the Nara period. There is, however, a small statue of him nearby, sitting in a recess in a wall, holding a scroll in his left hand.

Next to it is a row of other stone statues wearing white bibs, dedicated to the memory of those who died while undertaking severe religious training on Mt. Omine.

This mountain, a UNESCO World Heritage site, is considered to be holy. It has been used for a thousand years as a spiritual training ground by the Shugendo Buddhist sect, founded in the eighth century by En no Gyoja, (also called En no Ozuno and Jinben Daibosatsu, (ca 603–706 C.E.). To the right of the waterfall is a small wooden shrine dedicated to him.

Shugendo means "the way of training and testing", and there are elements of Shinto, Taoism, Tantrism, esoteric Buddhism, and Shamanism incorporated in it. These severe trials are usually undertaken by those referred to as *yamabushi* or *gyojya*—mountain ascetic hermits.

The mountain itself, like the *sumo* ring, has been off limits to women for 1,300. It has been suggested that this is not for reasons associated with menstrual impurity, but in order to protect them from bears, falling rocks, and other dangers. Women might also prove an unwelcome distraction to the *yamabushi*. The ban applied until the 1960s, though parts of the mountain are still forbidden to women. There are no penalties for violators, but visitors are requested to respect the ancient tradition.

These are the three tests of courage on Mt. Omine. The first is 'The Hanging Stone' or 'Crab Rock' (named because the climber looks like a crab when climbing)—a 30-foot cliff with an overhang at the top. The climber is required to swing out over the overhang using an embedded length of chain. It is not clear if the chain has always been available as an aid, or was attached later to prevent fatal accidents.

Next is 'The Insight from the West'—a sheer cliff about 200 feet high. Disciples and serious believers are held head-first over the cliff by their ankles and expected to confess their faults in response to questions, and to promise to obey social and religious laws.

Finally, 'The Rock of Equality' is a rock tower overlooking a steep cliff. Projections from the wall allow the believer to travel from one side to the other. This test is available only by special request.

At first, En no gyoja lived on Mt. Katsuragi, and was acclaimed for his magic powers, being able to manipulate demons into drawing water and gathering firewood. When he tried to order the demons to build a bridge between Mt. Kongo and Mt. Katsuragi, this angered the mountain god of Mt. Katsuragi, (Hitokoto nushi), who took human form and slandered him to Emperor Mommu. He was then exiled to the Izu islands on June 29th, 699 C.E., from which he was released on January 1st 701 C.E. He is also credited with being the first Ommyo-ji, (diviner, spell-caster, and fortune teller).

Ommyo-do (the way of Yin and Yang combined with the five elements of wind, water, fire, earth, and metal) became a central part of Japanese culture. Fortune-telling techniques were thought to be able to serve human needs and were based on auspicious and inauspicious signs seen in nature.

Ommyo-do came to include *katata-gae* (how to reach a destination by a circuitous route without going directly from one's own house, and by staying somewhere else the night before), *monoimi* (fasting, abstinence, and confinement to one's house on an unlucky day), *henbai* (the art of public entertainment using special footsteps believed to have magical powers), *taizanfukunnsai* (a spirit-exchange ritual), *fusuisetu*, and *jukon-do* (a medical art), *juho* (self-discipline by uttering mantras), and *sukuyo-do* (astrology).

In 1872 the Meiji government also abolished Ommyo-do as a superstition, but its vestiges remain in the modern Japanese calendar, which still displays lucky and unlucky days, and for those who observe special directions for important events. The popular, eponymous Seimei shrine in *Kyoto* is dedicated to a famous tenth-century Ommyo-ji.

We return to the shrine's regular path. On either side of two sets of stone steps are small mounds of sand with a sprig of *sasaki* stuck in them to allow the descent of *kami*, as at Kamigamo shrine. A magnificent pine tree on the right stands guard.

These steps lead up to the main shrine from which hang two purple curtains displaying the Imperial sixteen-petalled chrysanthemum. We clap our hands, bow our heads, and pay our respects.

A Zen teacher of mine once told me that we can never see the *kami* whom we summon, because they appear only at the moment our heads are bowed, but that it is the reverential bowing of the head which is important, not the seeing of the *kami*.

One of the delights of Kyoto is that exploration frequently leads to hidden discoveries which open up surprising, new perspectives on the city, its history, and those who lived and died there centuries ago. You never know when you turn a corner whether you will once again be stumbling into the tenth century or standing on a spot where an important historical event which irrevocably altered the future of the country took place.

Kyoto is a city of memories only slightly hidden from view, and it is to the credit of the local authorities that they keep these memories alive with explanatory signboards for the benefit of curious and ignorant visitors such as ourselves.

Like the intertwining roots of the shrine's great trees, the strands of history in Kyoto are all part of a vast interlinked web, so that Sudou shrine will forever remain a fascinating gateway into a long-vanished world.

※

**Malcom Ledger** was born in Belfast, UK, in 1948. He graduated from Trinity College of Music, London, and London University Institute of Education. He became interested in Zen Buddhism, joining a Zen Group under the instruction of Daiyu Myokyo Zenji (then, Ven. Myokyo Ni), before moving to Japan in 1977 to continue training. He was accepted as a disciple by Soko Morinaga Roshi at Daishuin (Ryoanji), and he also began to study the Way of Tea. He taught English in a Japanese high school for thirty-one years, retiring in 2014. He came late to writing. He lives in Takagamine, north-west Kyoto.

WRITERS IN KYOTO COMPETITION | KYOTO CITY 2022 MAYORAL PRIZE

# The Watcher

MARIA DANUCO

I noticed her house, long before I noticed her. It was a small building, falling apart at the seams, with its ramshackle roof sinking towards the earth while the overgrown garden reached for the heavens. A family of stray cats had made their home somewhere within the gates, and they glared at me with suspicion when I passed each day on my way to the station.

Perhaps back in its glory days it could have been a grand place. Given its proximity to the grounds of Kyoto Imperial Palace, it could have even been important. But now it was rotting—forgotten and abandoned.

Until the day she appeared.

I noticed her immediately; there is no way I wouldn't have. Her *kimono* was far too elegant for someone who lived in a house like that. And yet there she was, standing solemnly in the sagging doorway. From the shadows, she gazed out at the world and watched, and the world seemed to slide by her: cars, bicycles, people, me.

Days passed, and I never saw her do anything but watch.

Sometime later, I moved away and forgot about her until I returned during Golden Week. The house was gone. Perhaps the roof had finally worn out and sunk gratefully into the ground, crushing the hopeful plants beneath it. Just as likely, the owners, wherever they were, had been offered a fair sum and sold the land.

As I stood there, I was struck with a strange sense of mourning. I felt that a piece of history had been wiped away, but that wasn't unusual. Kyoto was going bankrupt, and history doesn't pay the bills the same way parking lots can.

I thought of her—of all she had seen—and I wondered if, somehow, she'd known what was coming all along.

※

**Maria Danuco** is a writer of Filipino/Australian descent born on unceded Noongar land in the southwest of Western Australia. She has lived in Tokyo since 2019. An avid reader, traveller and recovering teacher, Maria spends most of her time these days writing, baking and pursuing whatever new hobby has piqued her interest.

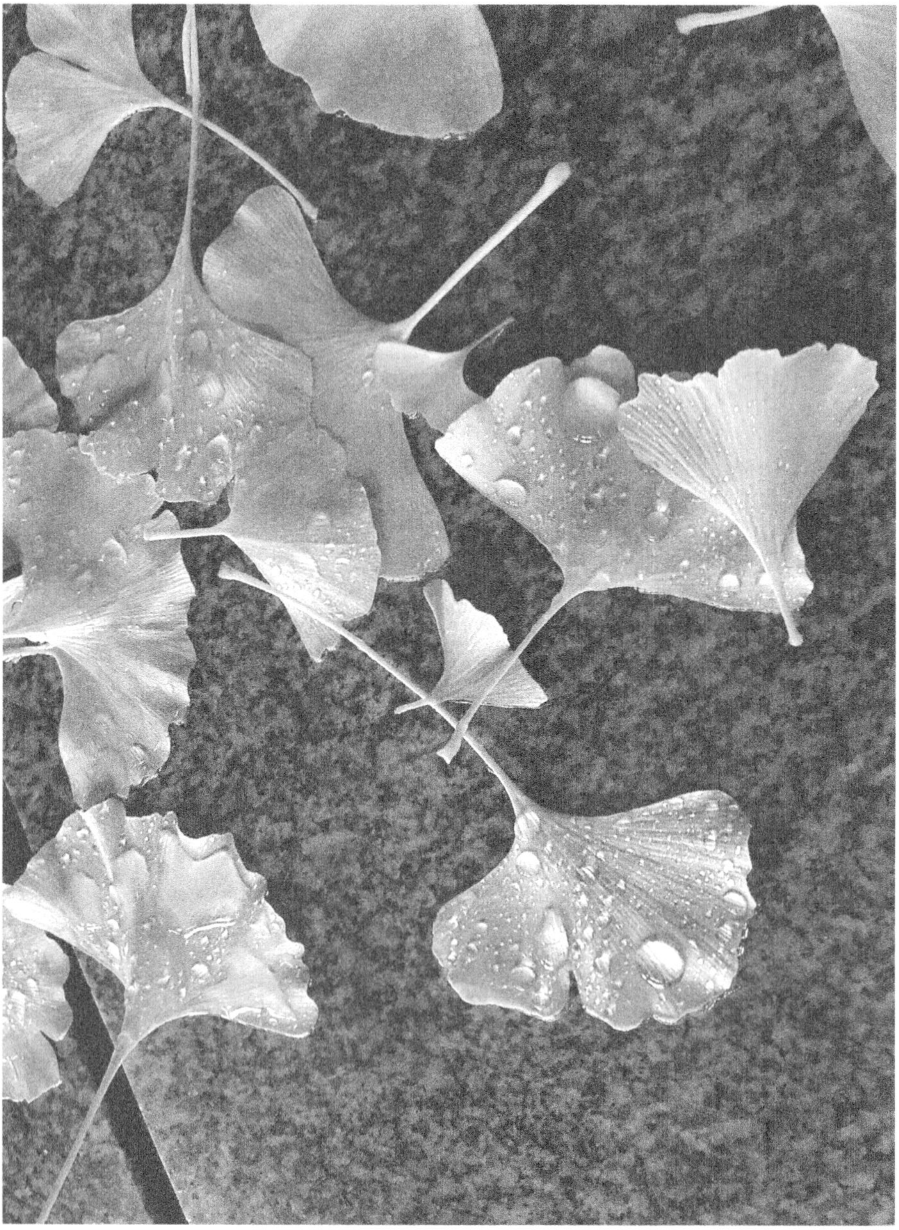

# "Keywords" of Kyoto

MAYUMI KAWAHARADA

## 桜 (Sakura) — Cherry tree

Naked cherry trees —
Pink branches, silver branches
Bathed in sunlight

Swelling cherry buds
Change from brown to pink —
Rain for the flowers

## 筍 (Takenoko) — Bamboo shoots

Cracks in a concrete path
Made by bamboo shoots pushing up —
"Whack-a-mole" game

Field of bamboo shoots
Gives the scarecrow work —
An April shower

## 川 (Kawa) — River

In a twinkling
Ripples spread over the river —
Torrential rainfall

Striped sheets of water deluge
From the eaves of the riverside café —
Fat dripping raindrops

## 汗 (Ase) — Sweat

Polka-dot design
Drowned on my white hiking T-shirt —
Drips of sweat

## 紅葉 (Koyo) — Autumn leaves

Autumn mountains
Reflected in the river —
A rainbow!

Yellow carpets
Gone with the wind —
Bare Gingko trees

## 底冷え (Sokobie) — Raw winter

Slanting light snow
Conceals the mountains —
Ink painting world

After harsh cold days
With the first storm of spring,
Buds awaken at once

※

**Mayumi Kawaharada** grew up, lives and works in Kyoto. She started writing *haiku* in English in 2004, as a member of the Hailstone Haiku Circle. She self-published the bilingual *haiku* and photo booklet *Three and half years passed in Fukushima* (2015). Her work appears in anthologies and websites of the Haiku Circle, Writers in Kyoto and Haiku Spirit.

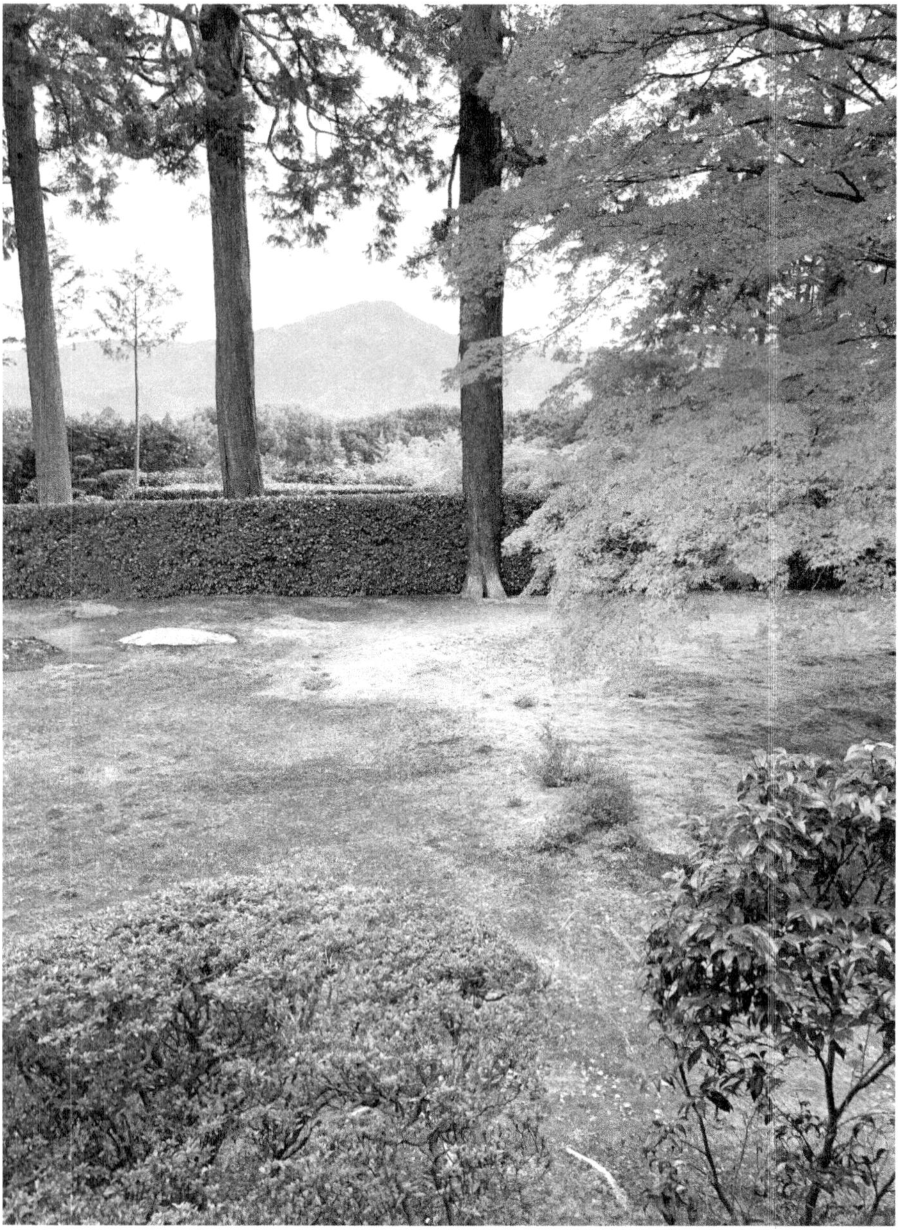

# The Hills of Kyoto

PATRICK COLGAN

'Fosco Maraini? He was just an *otaku* of his time and a womanizer. What else?'

I listen to Lorenzo and feel like interrupting him. *Otaku*—someone with obsessive, consuming interests—is not necessarily an offensive word, but his intention is clear. This insult to the great Florentine writer, scholar, and photographer hurts me. Let's be objective: Maraini was a little more than that: he documented the life of the Ainu in the early 1900s, lived in Kyoto for years before the war, studied Japanese history and culture, and was detained for a long time in a prison camp with his family for his refusal to adhere to fascism; famously, he cut off his little finger and threw it to the Japanese guards to save his family from starvation.

Moreover, Maraini's books have accompanied me on my travels in Japan as if they were the voice of an older and more experienced companion, a wry and stern teacher telling me stories about a Japan that no longer exists. I think I owe a debt to him.

But I listen in silence, partly because Lorenzo is a river in flood. And I've only known him for a few minutes, after all. I walked into The Gael pub at the end of a long evening walk along the Kamogawa, looking for a beer and someone to chat with. Once inside, I recognized Andrea, a fellow Italian guy who lives in Kyoto and whom I knew only online. He had a blog, and we had exchanged a few messages in the past. He was with what looked like three other Italians, and it seemed like an absurd coincidence; what were the odds? There are people in my town, much smaller than Kyoto, whom I haven't met in 20 years. I was paralysed for a few seconds as I watched him and felt as if I were looking at another life I was living in Kyoto in a parallel universe, the one I never dared to imagine.

I approached them in Italian, and after their initial surprise, they invited me to join them. We introduced ourselves. They were at the pub for a jazz concert, and they had never been to it before. The band was on a break, and the singer, possibly an American, was drinking at the bar with a Japanese girl, not far from us. Before I could even open my mouth, Lorenzo took the floor to tell me what the ancient capital really was. Perhaps he thought it was my first time in the city and he warned me: 'Don't trust the appearances, the temples and gardens. They are for tourists. Kyoto is dead and, at its heart, is a narrow-minded, mean, inaccessible city. It is a city of merchants who only care about money. When I go to Osaka, I feel like I can breathe'.

His rant has been going on for a few minutes now. I keep listening to him and wondering why he continues to live in Kyoto. But I am used to this kind of talk from foreigners, exasperated and attracted to Japan at the same time. I am just a visitor, and I listen—and deep down, I admire those who have managed to settle in this city, to live here. Sometimes our love for a place makes us harsh in our judgments. I feel despair in his words.

As the night ends, I say goodbye to the four guys, and we promise to keep in touch. And as I walk to the *ryokan* along the Takase River, I think about my connection to Kyoto, the stinging nostalgia I feel when I leave and, absurdly, when I return: a delusion, no doubt, which makes me feel at home as soon as its hills appear from the Shinkansen. It's a sense of comfort, peace, and belonging that rests on nothing besides my memories and feelings. The hills announce the gardens, the temples, the quiet alleys, the shops, restaurants and bars that I like, my friends, they remind me of the emotions of my first trip. But I also see my face reflected in the train's glass window; it looks like that of a ghost suspended among the hills. That's how I feel.

Sometimes I imagine that the train does not glide swiftly between the buildings on the outskirts of Kyoto and then quickly into its gargantuan station but, instead, enters a vast, grass-covered plain mirroring a huge blue sky, surrounded on three sides by the green, continuous, undulating profile of the hills. Once, perhaps,

Higashiyama, Kitayama, and Nishiyama could all be taken in with a single glance. Perhaps that was what the emperor had seen around 1,200 years ago: a natural defensive structure, a fortress, as it was described at the time, which was the official motivation for choosing the city's location. But I wonder if maybe he had been enraptured by the beauty of the place, akin to a welcoming, maternal womb where he thought he could build a capital that would exist forever? The beautiful hills probably looked very much as they do today: mute witnesses to history as the incredible city was built, destroyed, and rebuilt again and again. They had seen the rise and fall of magnificent temples, the madness and cruelty of wars, and they were indifferent to it all. And even more so to me now.

Not only Emperor Kammu, but also anyone who lived in Kyoto—from Murasaki Shikibu to Fosco Maraini—saw the same hills and mountains unchanged. They have always been part of the city and its scenery. Not all cities have this privilege. Tokyo's valleys, rivers, and its early 1600s landscape are buried under layers of concrete and asphalt. They can only be guessed from ancient descriptions or by paying attention to the land's ups and downs, and the location of shrines, temples and gardens. In old Edo the distant Fuji-san could be seen from different areas, while now, when not concealed by mists and clouds, it's mostly obscured by buildings and skyscrapers. Kyoto, on the other hand, still has Mount Hiei in sight. Hills appear in the distance along the river, on bridges, behind temples, and down streets.

It is said that almost nothing remains of the ancient Heian-Kyo. This is partly true, but the hills are still here, and they are deeply interconnected with the city. Their water, air, and presence are part of Kyoto. As John Dougill wrote, 'We think of ourselves as separate from mountains, but in a very real sense, we're not. The hills are us'.

I search for the texts in which Maraini described the hills of Kyoto, and find just a few emotional paragraphs. In *Meeting with Japan*, he quotes the 'purple hills' and his 'beloved hillocks,' while in his biography, he describes the outlines of the hills he saw from the second floor of his old house that reminded him of those around

Florence. He lived in Asukai-cho, which in Italian he had translated as the 'Village of the flying bird's well' (飛鳥井町). Strangely, this name doesn't appear in the English version of the book.

The following morning, I take the subway to Demachiyanagi, get off and observe the bifurcation of the Kamogawa. I love this place, where the water takes up space; it feels as if Kyoto opens like a book, the sky feels bigger, and the Kitayama hills are so close that you feel you could quickly slide into their shady valleys and fresh streams. Asukai-cho is near the university area, north of the Chion-ji or Hyakuman-ben temples. I don't have any reference point other than Maraini's words: he says that to get to his house in 1939, he went through the temple area, exiting through a secondary door, and the house was there, not far from the wall. Every now and then, he would hear the notes of a *shakuhachi* flute master who lived next door. And from his window, he could see the hills between the temple roof and a 'sweet confusion of pine trees.' I think there can't be any view more emblematic of the ancient capital.

Maraini had returned after the war and found his former house, but not the people and ties he had left there, except for one of the neighbours. I never thought I would find that house again today, or any trace of it, after so many years and great changes in the city. In fact, the whole neighbourhood seems newly built. As I walk along the temple wall, edged by new houses with car parking areas, I look for a restaurant or store that has an upper floor, to recapture at least the view described by Maraini, but I can't find one. Young boys on the street are perhaps students, headed to the nearby university. I am thinking of heading back when I eventually catch a glimpse of a mountain among the low houses to the east. I stop for a moment as I want to remember this view and try to picture how the city could have been one hundred years ago. And I seem to see the tall figure of Fosco, walking east, right ahead of me.

*Notes: The Gael pub closed in 2017; Fosco Maraini was born in Florence in 1912, where he died in 2004. His travelogue* Meeting with Japan *was first published in English by Viking books in 1960. Some names and details have been changed to protect the privacy of the people involved.*

※

**Patrick Colgan** is an Italian newspaper journalist and travel writer born in Bologna, Italy, in 1978. His rendezvous with Japan happened by chance, but it was an undoubtable case of hopeless love at first sight; exploring the country, studying its culture, and learning the language became an obsession for him. He writes about his travels and Japan in his Italian-language blog *Orizzonti*. He also published several travelogues and guides in Italy as well as stories for newspapers and magazines such as *National Geographic Traveler*. Patrick is one of three authors of the new Japan guidebook by the leading Italian publisher, Touring Editore.

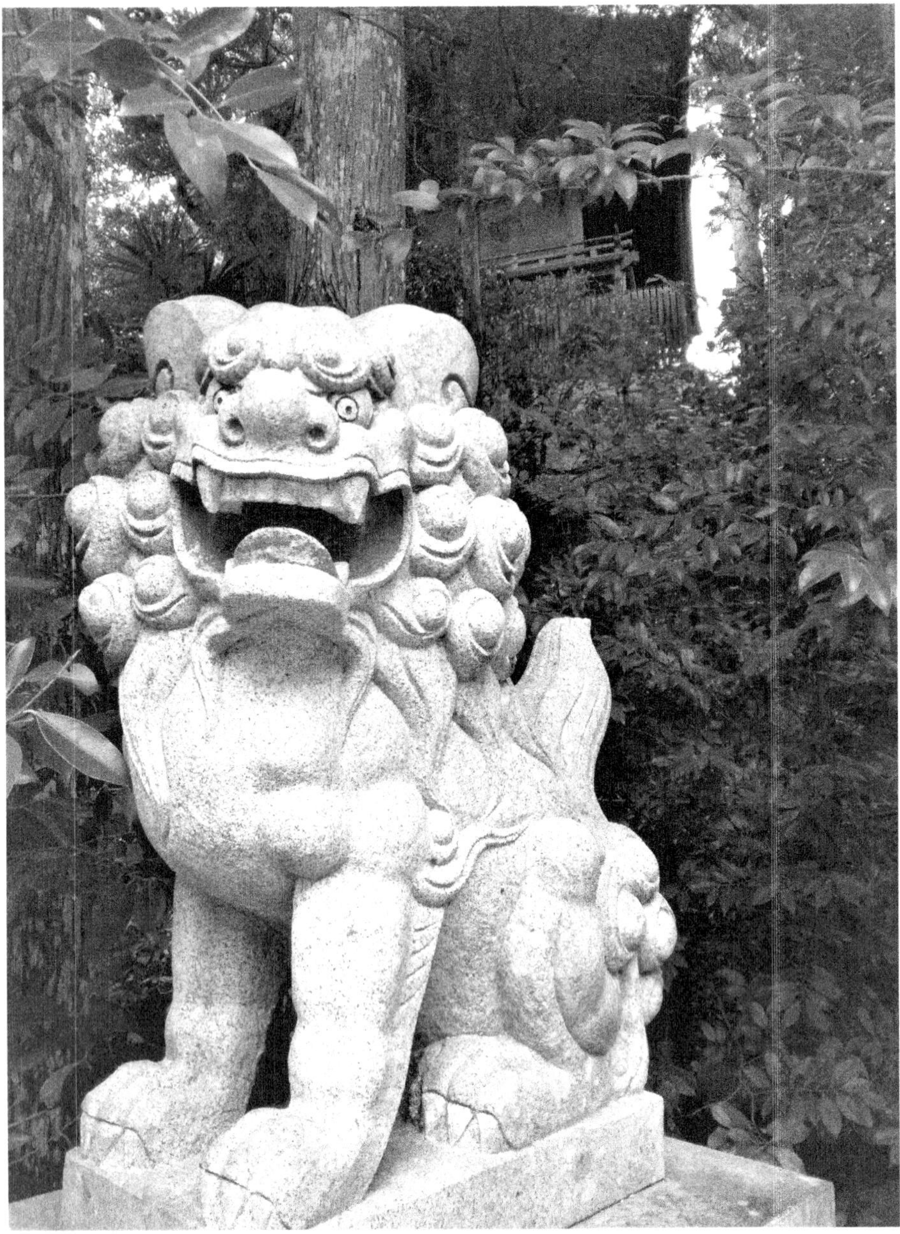

# Kyotoyana

PRESTON KEIDO HOUSER

Travel brings the notion of a personal "homestead" into question and few destinations instigate this challenge more than Japan's ancient capital. Kyoto is popularly considered a place to visit at least once in one's life (a "bucket-list" goal, to employ the vulgar vernacular) and travelers often arrive to discover a feeling of having lived here in the past—or, as John Denver once sang, of "coming home to a place [they've] never been before."

A Taoist or Buddhist might propose that Kyoto is a way to No-Way; for example, those who find their way to Kyoto have actually exemplified the archetype of the Way, connoting that the approach to a sacred site is as significant as the entrance. The exterior of the temple or shrine represents *samsara*, the daily grind of birth and death, while the interior of a temple, to extend the metaphor, is consciousness. Passing the guardian deities (*niou*) or beasts (*koma-inu*) or entering through a *torii* gate, the pilgrim leaves the secular world behind and demonstrates a commitment to spiritual endeavor. Likewise, Kyoto is not a city in which to reside so much as to travel through—the natural experience of most wayfarers who come to Kyoto, either by transport or birth. Even in *The Avatamsaka Sutra*, legendary sage Muktaka advises Sudhana that "travel means not dwelling." In many respects, anyone who has visited Kyoto has been, for all intents and purposes, "born" here, since the city appears to qualify as a spiritual point of departure.

Two major paradigms of Buddhism, the Mahayana and Hinayana, denote paths to understanding and realization. Without implying notions of superiority or inferiority, these two religious courses are responses to cultural conditions rather than dogma. They are, as their suffixes suggest, vehicles (*yana*). The Mahayana, the "greater vehicle," evokes China, Korea, and Japan, while the Hinayana, the "lesser vehicle" (or Theravada: the "way of the elders"), conjures up images of Southeast Asia. To oversimplify, Mahayana Buddhists are characterized by living in the world while not being "of the world," exercising an altruistic socialism; on the other hand, Hinayana Buddhists are thought to be "of the world" but not living in it, having retired from secular life in order to perfect themselves in isolation. Both paths are beneficial in their ways, their *yana*. The suffix *yana* also appears in the practices of *Vajrayana* ("thunderbolt vehicle"), *tantrayana* ("transformation"), and *mantrayana* ("recitation of sacred syllables") — routes to enlightenment. *Yana*, nearly synonymous with *dharma*, is a means, a vehicle, a method, a practice of the tantric arts. In this respect, Kyoto, as a city and a cultural force, also qualifies as a means or route to heightened, if not concluding, consciousness.

The "journey to end all journeys" is not an easy one, although water can ease the commute. Indeed, representations of water, rivers, and oceans permeate Buddhist and Taoist lore. Traditionally, the river is a narrative symbol of ceaseless flow and change, like the *taiji* or yin-yang. Although Kyoto is land-locked, images of water are essential elements of the city. The Kamo River and Takano River pass through Kyoto but, rather than dividing it, they reaffirm the city as an enormous metaphysical river containing all rivers and, to extend the meta-narrative, as a text containing all texts. Heraclitus suggested that no one ever steps in the same river twice. T.S. Eliot considered the river a strong brown god, "sullen, untamed and intractable." The Sanzu River, in Japanese mythology, is the river all souls must cross to realize the afterlife.

Moreover, Herman Hesse included the tale of Siddhartha, the river, and the ferryman in his eponymous novel of the Buddha. The ferry and the ferryman extend and clarify the Buddhist metaphors of the *bodhisattva* and spiritual journey. A symbol of sympathy, the ferryman navigates the incessant flux of *samsara*, taking Siddhartha across to the "other shore"—itself a metaphor for enlightened compassion (*nirvana*). The *bodhisattva* ideal consists of an individual who has glimpsed the other shore but who postpones personal salvation in order to help others across the river, i.e. a ferryman. In this regard, Hinayana Buddhists often refer to the *dharmakaya*, the inconceivable body of the Buddha that serves as a "raft" to *nirvana*, the enlightened shore. (The word *dharma* is usually translated as law or, more accurately, as a means or vehicle, thus a "law of nature" as opposed to coarse jurisprudence. The word *kaya* simply means body.) *Bodhisattvas* remain on the proverbial ferry, transporting pilgrims across the water, which is to say, they choose to reside in "Kyoto consciousness" and offer guidance and comfort to the hapless visitor.

Philosopher Alan Watts envisioned Kyoto as comprising two powerful images: first, as the incarnation of the *bodhisattva* Kannon and second, as a mandala or *manji* rather than a territorial terminus. Consider, for example, the androgynous god of mercy, Kannon (aka Avalokiteshvara in Sanskrit and Guanyin in Chinese), the one who harkens to the sorrows of the world, often portrayed as a multi-faced and multi-handed saint representing the particular details of worldly existence, the pitiable polarities and dastardly dualities. At the same time, Kannon is easily regarded as a singular presence that embodies a sacred awareness of the holistic sphere, pointing to an all-encompassing Kyoto as a kind of urban *bodhisattva*, capable of reflecting the myriad details of its neighborhoods, temples and shrines, gardens and shopping districts. Simultaneously, Kyoto, when viewed as a mandala, enables a larger view of the holy unity of life and reality—what some environmentalists acknowledge as the cosmic perfection of the natural world, a perfection that will outlive the destructive pettiness of human endeavor. Kyoto, more than a mere destination, is greater than the culmination of countless individual projections; it is a vessel that contains the aesthetic wishes of the whole world. This is the vision that Alan Watts perceived.

Furthermore, Kyoto adumbrates the very nature of a spiritual transformation. For example, *The Heart Sutra*—a primary text for Buddhists everywhere, for the Mahayana as well as Hinayana traditions alike—concludes with the mantra *gate gate paragate parasamgate,* which usually translates as "gone" or "to go beyond" (*gate*) to the further shore (*para*). The further shore is believed to encompass both form and emptiness, a body interdependent on all things and, when the traveler has "arrived," the experience is of *nirvana*. My personal interpretation is that the word *gate* is actually a contronym which denotes coming and going, simultaneously departing and arriving—not in a linear sense but as a cyclic mandala or *manji*. Visiting Kyoto is like embarking on a gyroscopic mandala that enlightens without "deliverance" (*gate gate*).

To borrow Gertrude Stein's wry observation concerning Oakland, California, that "there's no there there," the received Kyoto City image of former pilgrims, globe trotters, expatriates, and countless travel agents do, in fact, promise a "there there." Tourists who visit Kyoto and return home to sing its praises as the global goal of choice have, unfortunately, transformed this miraculous metropolis into an exit-less cul-de-sac. In this sense, for centuries, Kyoto has been a victim of rampant metro-idolatry, given to rotating epochs of Heian glory and Onin devastation. (The temporal purity or dereliction of Kyoto is really no one's concern, except for the self-proclaimed custodians of cultural virtue.) Travelers who return home after visiting Kyoto in the belief that they have actually *been* somewhere quickly realize that they have not been "over the rainbow," that there was no pot of gold, and they invariably begin to plan their next sojourn, perhaps to the next cultural "hot spot," another installment in the perpetual pursuit of destinations, collecting landmarks like so many decals on luggage—such is the frustrated travel consumer.

Buddhism stresses a life of non-attachment as a way to relieve suffering. An attachment to Kyoto as a sacred place or center of the metaphysical world is a tender temptation. A commentary on *The Gandavyuha*, the final book of *The Avatamsaka Sutra*, is crystal clear on this point: Having once crossed a river, one does not continue to carry the boat on land. Ironically, for intrepid transients, after Kyoto's "thereness" becomes a "hereness," the city points to a further "thereness" to be explored (*gate gate*), albeit an exploration of consciousness.

Leonard Cohen once questioned if "travel leads us anywhere;" Paul Bowles claimed that the traveler belongs "no more to one place than the next;" a popular aphorism suggests that to "travel is better than to arrive"—we arrive on earth, like King Lear, knowing that we're only passing through this "great stage of fools." Coming to the great stage of Kyoto, the wanderer is made aware, not of a disillusionment of destination, but rather of a re-illumination of travel. The perceptive pilgrim can see Kyoto for what it is: a vehicle, not a destination. Like our personal, carnal body, which we occupy only temporarily, Kyoto is a collective body to be eventually discarded. We are only passing through, negotiating a mundane menagerie of personal details with the existential awe of the universe. In spite of a wayfarer's wishful thinking, Kyoto is not the "other shore;" on the contrary, Kyoto is the *yana*, the ferry.

If a travel narrative teaches vagabonds anything, the moral of the story is that the concept of destination is precarious. The fortuitous pilgrim comes to realize that incessant coming-and-going (*gate gate*) is futile as well. For astute tourists who make the trek to Kyoto, the observer and the observed quickly become a single entity and then, as Zen masters Huangbo Xiyun and Bankei Yotaku might suggest, there is no return from the "no-there." This mini-epiphany transcends departure-and-arrival, and travel becomes the arrival of no-arrival at the destination of no-destination—not a nihilistic nowhere but a hylozoistic now-here.

Voilà! The nature of *Kyotoyana*!

❋

**Preston Keido Houser** came to Kyoto in 1981 to pursue his interests in Zen Buddhism and traditional Japanese music, specifically the Zen repertoire for the *shakuhachi* bamboo flute as played by the *komuso* monks of the Fuke-shu sect. He earned his master's license, took the name Keido, and performs frequently in Japan and America. An award-winning writer and poet, Preston has authored several books on Japanese gardens.

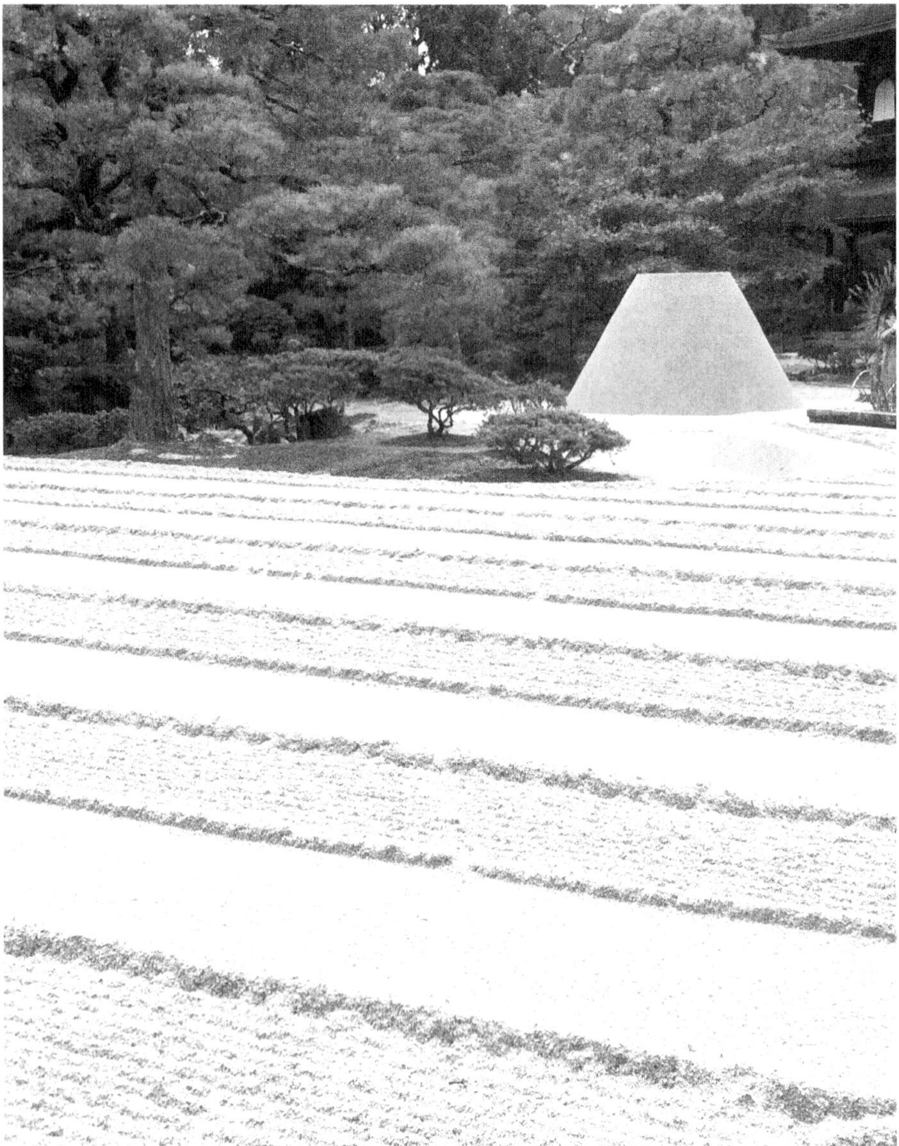

# Thinking Kyoto like a Mountain

ROBERT WEIS

'Thinking like a mountain' is a term coined by American author and ecologist Aldo Leopold in his book *A Sand County Almanac*. For Leopold, thinking like a mountain means having a holistic appreciation of the deep interconnectedness of the elements of ecosystems, rather than thinking as an isolated individual. This full appreciation of interdependent relationships is what opened my eyes and heart to seeing Kyoto as a special place on this planet, a connecting point between land- and mindscapes, outer and inner worlds.

As the French writer Paul Claudel emphasized, in Japan, nature and the supernatural are one. Kyoto's nature contains a spiritual dimension: looking at Kyoto means *seeing* the invisible among the visible. The mountains are a particular component of the earthly and mental landscape; as a physical barrier, they prevent a complete view of the horizon. What is visible is always only a part of it; to discover more, to make another point of view one's own, one has to make the effort to climb that mountain, only to find oneself facing an even bigger mountain that obstructs your view and by doing so obliges you to take a deep look inside. This is the essence of the mountain pilgrimage, a true spiritual quest driven by the hope of one day seeing a free horizon by looking within. Dutch travel writer Cees Noteboom concludes in his report on the Saigoku, the 33 temple pilgrimage around Kyoto: 'Anyone who has never climbed temples and monasteries in the mountains does not know what a sense of satisfaction and comfort it brings'.

My idea of Kyoto exists through the mountains that surround it, just as our very souls exist through the body that envelops them: mountains dreamed of, mountains celebrated in poetry and painting, mountains revered and held in awe as the seat of the *kami*, the Shinto deities and ancestral spirits. The ancient name of Japan is Yamato, which today translates as 'great harmony'; the ancient meaning, however, is said to be different: Yamato would have meant 'the passage through the mountains', a clear reference to Japan's rugged morphology and the central role that the mountain imaginary occupies. For the Japanese, the mountain is the object of veneration par excellence. Fuji-san (3776 m) is a national symbol and every Japanese person who respects tradition dreams of climbing it at least once in their life. The ascent of the mountain symbolises the spiritual steps to be taken before reaching the summit, i.e. enlightenment. In the ancient Japan of the feudal lords, *kunimi* ('looking at the kingdom') was a widespread tradition: on auspicious days, rulers would go to the highest points of their domains to look at the land they ruled in order to give blessings for good harvests.

Pilgrimage and religious practice in the mountains have a long history in Japan. The *yamabushi* (mountain ascetic hermits) in particular, surrounded by a mysterious aura, stayed in the mountains for spiritual purposes. An old Japanese saying states, 'You don't go to the mountains to be awakened. Rather, you go there because you are awake'. Other reasons for venturing into the mountains were poetic walks to admire the moon and flowers, or to gather wild vegetables and other medicinal herbs.

Mountaineering in the Western sense has developed in Japan only recently. An emblematic figure of Japanese mountaineering is Kyuya Fukada, the author of *Nihon Hyakumazei* (*The Hundred Mountains of Japan*). These 100 peaks represent Fukada's personal definition of a remarkable mountain: one whose ascent presents a certain interest, but also scenic qualities such as the view from the summit, as well as religious-spiritual associations. He believes a mountain worthy of the name should have character, a rich history and ideally exceed 1500 m in altitude. According to Fukada,

'Nowhere in the world do people hold mountains in higher esteem than in Japan. Mountains have played a role in Japanese history since the country's beginnings and are manifested in all forms of art. Indeed, mountains have always been the foundation of the Japanese soul'.

Kyoto is surrounded on three sides by low and undulating mountains, namely the Higashiyama, Kitayama and Nishiyama mountain ranges, which offer multiple vistas to anyone venturing into the city. These elevations are an inescapable attraction for the intrigued journeymen, with countless trails to explore their mysterious beauty as a backdrop to the landscape of the urban area. The foothills are home to historic structures such as shrines and temples, including the World Heritage Sites for which Kyoto is famous. Scenic sites abound in Kyoto, which is known as the city of *sanshi-suimei* or "purple mountains and clear waters'.

Making your way through these purple mountains—or, in other words, *living your own way through the mountains*—takes some time; in my case, this exploration is linked to a number. The number six has always brought me luck. I was six years old when the world opened up, like a flower after a spring rain: my first books, my first natural history collections (it all started with a few dozen devil's claws from the field near my great-grandmother's house), my first writing experiences. Six is also the number of my very personal selection of mountains that embody the spirit of Kyoto as I perceive it through my intimate experience. The six are, from northwest to southeast: Mount Ogura, Mount Atago, Mount Kurama, Mount Hiei, Mount Daimonji, Mount Inari.

So where to start? The most obvious way would be to begin with Kyoto's most famous tourist destinations: Ginkakuji—the Silver Pavilion—for a quick climb up Daimonji Hill; or Fushimi Inari Shrine, with its myriad of shiny red *torii* gates leading to the top of Mount Inari; or Mount Ogura, along the bamboo grove and gardens of Okachi Sanso Villa in Arashiyama. These relatively easy climbs were my gateway to the mysterious world of the mountains surrounding Kyoto during my very first visits there. Later, when I returned for longer stays, I ventured on more challenging walks on the slopes of Mount Kurama to the north of the city, Mount Atago near Takao, and Mount Hiei. The latter two in particular are worlds apart, two sacred peaks that have always protected Kyoto and its people. The Buddhist Mount Hiei wards off evil spirits from the northeast, and its location was connected with the decision to build Kyoto in the valley, along with other geomantic considerations. The Shinto Mount Atago protects the city and its inhabitants from fire. Mount Kurama, on the other hand, is known as the birthplace of the holistic healing art Reiki, and its mystical mountain temple of Kurama-dera and the surrounding forests are believed to be the dwelling place of the Great Tengu, a dreadful red-faced mountain demon who causes wars and natural disasters.

Mount Hiei is a true landmark of Northeast Kyoto, with its conical shape vaguely reminiscent of Japan's most symbolic mountain, Mount Fuji. When I think of Mount Hiei, I cannot help but picture its venerable silhouette overlooking the Entsu-ji temple grounds. The temple garden presents a perfect example of *shakkei*, the art of borrowed landscape: its Hieizan stands in the background of a masterful composition of moss, red maples and cryptomeria. Unlike the mighty Mount Hiei—decidedly an individualist among Kyoto's mountains—Mount Atago disappears into the middle of the Kitayama Mountain range between Kyoto and Kameoka. For a long time I had trouble recognising its uncharacteristic silhouette, which stands in the background of Togetsu Bridge. Mount Atago hides its game well, as it is the highest peak in Kyoto at 924 metres, while Hieizan is only 846 metres tall. However, the latter is still more popular with mainly Japanese tourists, as it is easily accessible thanks to its lift system that allows visitors to overcome the difference in altitude in a few minutes. By contrast, Atago-san is only accessible on foot, after a real pilgrimage of several hours, involving countless stairs. It is this necessary physical effort that makes Atago-san much less visited—and all the more desirable amongst maybe all of Kyoto mountains.

If someone asked me which of these six mountains I would recommend to visit if they could only choose one, I would paradoxically reply: don't go to the mountains to find the mountains. I would instead send them to Ginkakuji, the Silver Pavilion, at the foot of Mount Daimonji. Here, at the end of the dry garden known as the Sea of Silver Sand, rises a flat-topped pyramidal structure made out of sand; some visitors see it as an idealized representation of Mount Fuji. For my part, I see it as an aestheticized embodiment of the true nature of Kyoto: a depiction of a mountain as a mental landscape, with a message inside as whispered by songwriter Libby Roderick:

> 'Find the mountain deep within your heart;
> it is calling you back home'.

※

**Robert Weis** is a Luxembourg-born paleontologist and writer. His love for Japan and Kyoto makes him come back to the old capital once a year. He has been a contributor to Writers in Kyoto anthologies and *Kyoto Journal* since 2021. His first poem anthology *Rêves d'un mangeur de kakis* (Dreams of a persimmon eater) has been published in early 2023. He is interested in Zen Buddhism and *bonsai*.

WRITERS IN KYOTO COMPETITION | 2021 **FIRST PRIZE**

# Kyoto Time

STEPHEN BENFEY

First light rouses Shizuka from her *futon*. She dons an indigo *kimono*. Skirts and blouses are not for her. Maybe, if she had been an actress… Silly thought! Barefoot, she descends the ladder-steep staircase to her speck of a bar just off Pontocho.

Before breakfast every morning, she walks to Nishiki Tenmangu Shrine at the east end of Nishiki-Ichiba—the old market street north of Shijo Dori. There she prays to the god of business acumen. The shrine gates are locked at this hour but Shizuka has a key to the service entrance. The priest's wife is a friend from childhood.

Her rounded *zori* sandals tick an adagio tempo on the pavement. Ahead lies Kawaramachi Dori, one of Kyoto's main north-south thoroughfares. Later in the day, it will be jammed. But now, it is empty, silent.

Shizuka cherishes silence. She loves the hush of the tea ceremony. Silence nourishes her after the nights of music, talk, and laughter.

She steps out onto Kawaramachi—two lanes going south, then two more going north. No lights here, no crosswalk, no traffic. She reaches the first lane marker when an engine's whine rends the silence. She looks to her right. Two taxis are bearing down on her at full speed. Shizuka turns to face them. She bows deeply in apology—for being a nuisance, the nuisance of an older, quieter, slower Kyoto.

Shizuka relaxes, ready for the "other world." The cars roar past, their wheels a blur to either side. Shizuka stays bowed in their wake, her *kimono* still rustling as the exhaust clears.

Is this heaven? But nothing has changed! She rises, slowly. She can see all the way to the mountains.

The taxis have left her alive. Untouched, like the soul of the city itself, by time.

※

**Stephen Benfey**, fiction writer, copywriter, and father, lived in Kyoto during the '70s, attending college, helping a Japanese gardener, producing videos, and listening to Osaka blues bands. There, he met his future wife and began writing copy. After raising their children in Tokyo, the couple moved to their current home in a coastal hamlet on the Boso peninsula.

# The Promise

TETIANA KORCHUK

It has happened in our early dating days, when you still can't quite wrap your head around the thought that feelings are actually mutual. You feel drunk with love, almost feverish from every single thing going on in your head. Everything around you seems magical, full of hidden meaning and perfectly imperfect. Every day is almost like the night before Christmas, when the next day should be even happier than today, and you are ready to experience that happiness with every tiny cell of your body.

I was waiting for him at the Keihan station, our usual meeting spot, just to walk alongside the Kamogawa river, like many times before. At university class we recently started studying *The Tale of Genji*, and my thoughts were wandering, trying to imagine Kyoto of those times. For just a moment I felt like I could see it, petite young ladies in *kimono*, fishermen in large straw hats, black-haired, tanned children running around barefoot. Children's laughter sounded almost like a melody of colorful wind chimes, hanging near entrances of the riverside houses. I could even smell freshly cooked food, probably made by a mother waiting for her family to gather for dinner and felt the taste of tart green tea on my tongue.

That moment I spotted him finally approaching, tall and easily noticeable among others. My heart skipped a bit, and I immediately was brought back to reality. We held hands and started slowly walking our usual route, talking about everything and observing other couples sitting close to each other facing the river. Someone was practicing saxophone under one of the bridges, housewives were walking their cute fluffy Shiba dogs with round tails. As evening approached, groups of young people with music and drinks started gathering here and there. Near the station performers were advertising a fire show starting in a few minutes.

Suddenly I saw a nicely dressed elderly couple walking towards us in a traditional Japanese manner, the wife just two steps behind her husband's back. They were smiling and talking quietly.

"Would we also be walking here when we are in our seventies, what do you think?" asked I, immediately feeling a little nervous, as if my life depended on his answer.

"Sure, I can promise you that," he said. "But we will also be holding hands." He was smiling only with his dark eyes.

My heart was full. Full of love to that elderly couple, the slow waters of the Kamogawa, and cute Shiba dogs. Full of love to him.

※

**Tetiana Korchuk** is a translator, teacher, and author born and raised in Kyiv, Ukraine. She first arrived in Japan in 2014 as an exchange program participant. After graduating from Taras Shevchenko National University of Kyiv with a major in Japanese Language and Literature, she moved to Japan permanently in 2017. She now resides in Kobe, Hyogo Prefecture and enjoys learning about traditional Japanese culture, writing short stories, and cuddling with her Shiba dog named Sakura.

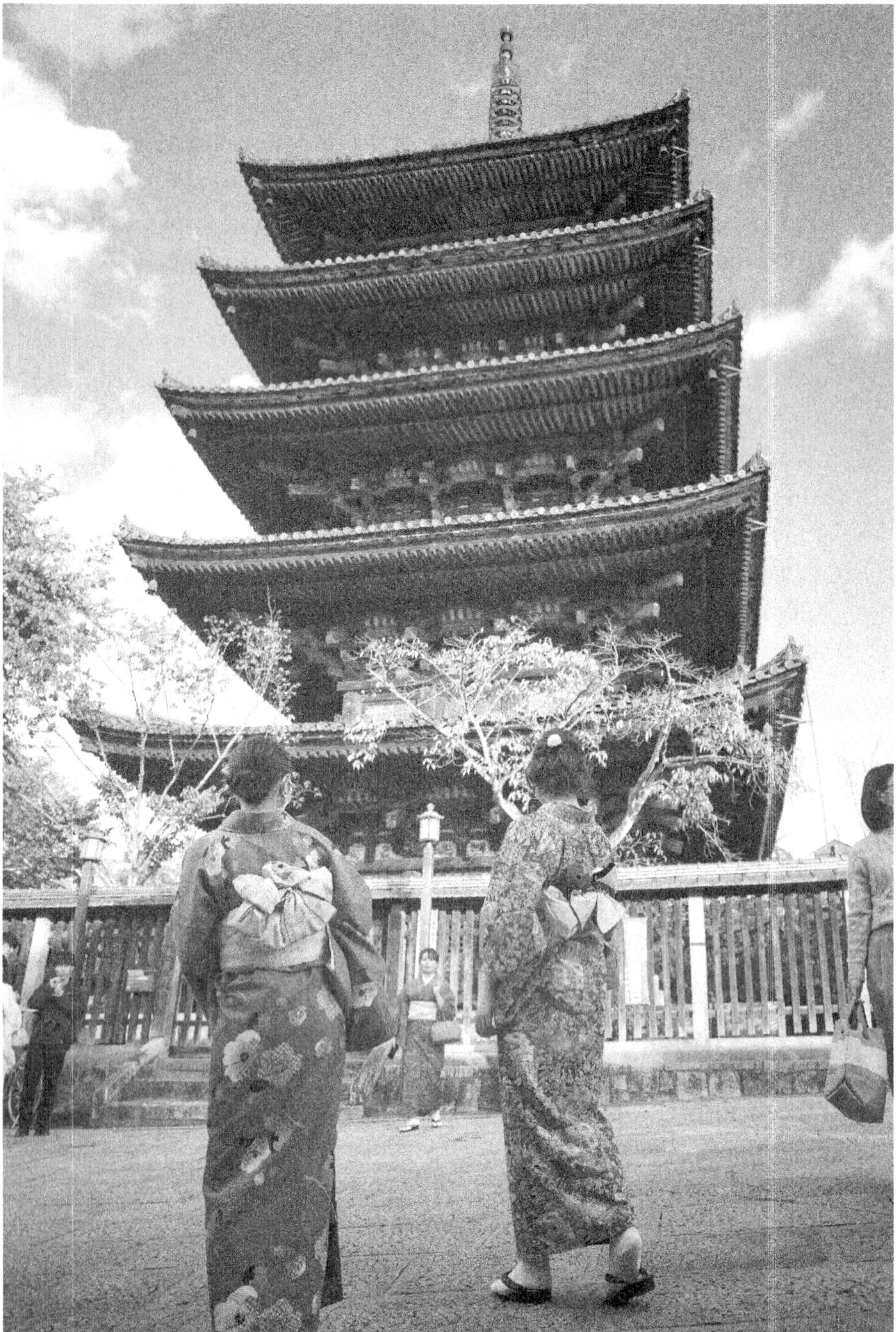

# Sound Travels

TINA DEBELLEGARDE

7,000 miles.
Unbridgeable this year.
I content myself with his phone calls.

His morning. My evening.
We share a yawn
as my ears follow him out his front door.

*Ohayou gozaimasu,*
I overhear my son say through the line.
His landlady swooshes her broom in response.

He stops at his favorite café.
Jazz competes with muffled chatter
and the squeal of steamed milk.

The wind rustles the trees.
It's snowing *sakura* petals, he says.
I close my eyes to see.

A bicycle bell trills at the intersection.
Now empty of tourists.
The chirp accompanies his crossing.

Through the temple grounds.
A clang. Then two claps.
I imagine a bowed head.

He coos to a cat in a narrow alley.
It turns, then scoots ahead.
Paws on pavement silent to us both.

The Kamo rushes past him.
An egret lands. It waits, watching for its dinner.
My son narrates in the silence.

Two girls walk by,
Chatting.
The high note of a giggle.

Are they flirting with him?
They press together in a whisper,
their voices lost to the current.

My morning. His evening.
It begins to rain. He opens his umbrella.
The patter louder now as it hits the dome above his head.

I wish you could see this, he whispers.
A Maiko slips out of a building,
a package cupped in her hands.

Doors swoosh. He enters the *conbini*.
The sing song *Irasshaimase*.
He pays with the drop of coins.

*Konbanwa*,
to his landlady once again.
I envision his silent bow.

The elevator door slides shut.
Halfway across the planet
I briefly lose the connection. Silence.

His keys jangle, his front door squeaks.
With the clang of the closing door,
We leave behind the sounds of Kyoto.

Slip, slip.
His shoes are off.
*Tadaima*

*For the thirty months that border restrictions were in place in Japan, I relied on sound travel. I became resourceful about staying connected to my son and to the unique city he has called home these last twelve years. During that time, the nature of Kyoto for me was the sounds which traveled over the phone line. Kyoto became its sounds. I clung to every chirp, whoosh and clap. To every jazz note, and every train announcement. Not having the other senses available to me, the sounds became more distinct, more precious, and transported me to Kyoto.*

*Upon the borders' re-opening, I finally set out to visit my son in November 2022. I discovered that those phone calls had altered my connection to the city. Distance has indeed made my heart grow fonder, but also it has forever enriched my sensory experience of Kyoto.*

※

**Tina deBellegarde** writes the Batavia-on-Hudson Mystery series. *Winter Witness* was nominated for the Agatha Award for Best First Novel. Her story "Tokyo Stranger" appeared in the 2021 *Mystery Writers of America* anthology and was nominated for a Derringer Award. Tina is the membership secretary of Writers in Kyoto. She lives in New York with her husband Denis and their cat Shelby where they tend bees and harvest *shiitake* mushrooms. Her latest passion is writing book reviews for *Books on Asia* (booksonasia.net). She is currently working on Book Three of her series set mostly in Kyoto.

京都総合観光案内所
Tourist Information
コインロッカー
Coin Lockers
エレベーター
Elevator
八条西口
Hachijō West Exit
タクシー
Taxi
新幹線
Shinkansen
近鉄電車
Kintetsu Line

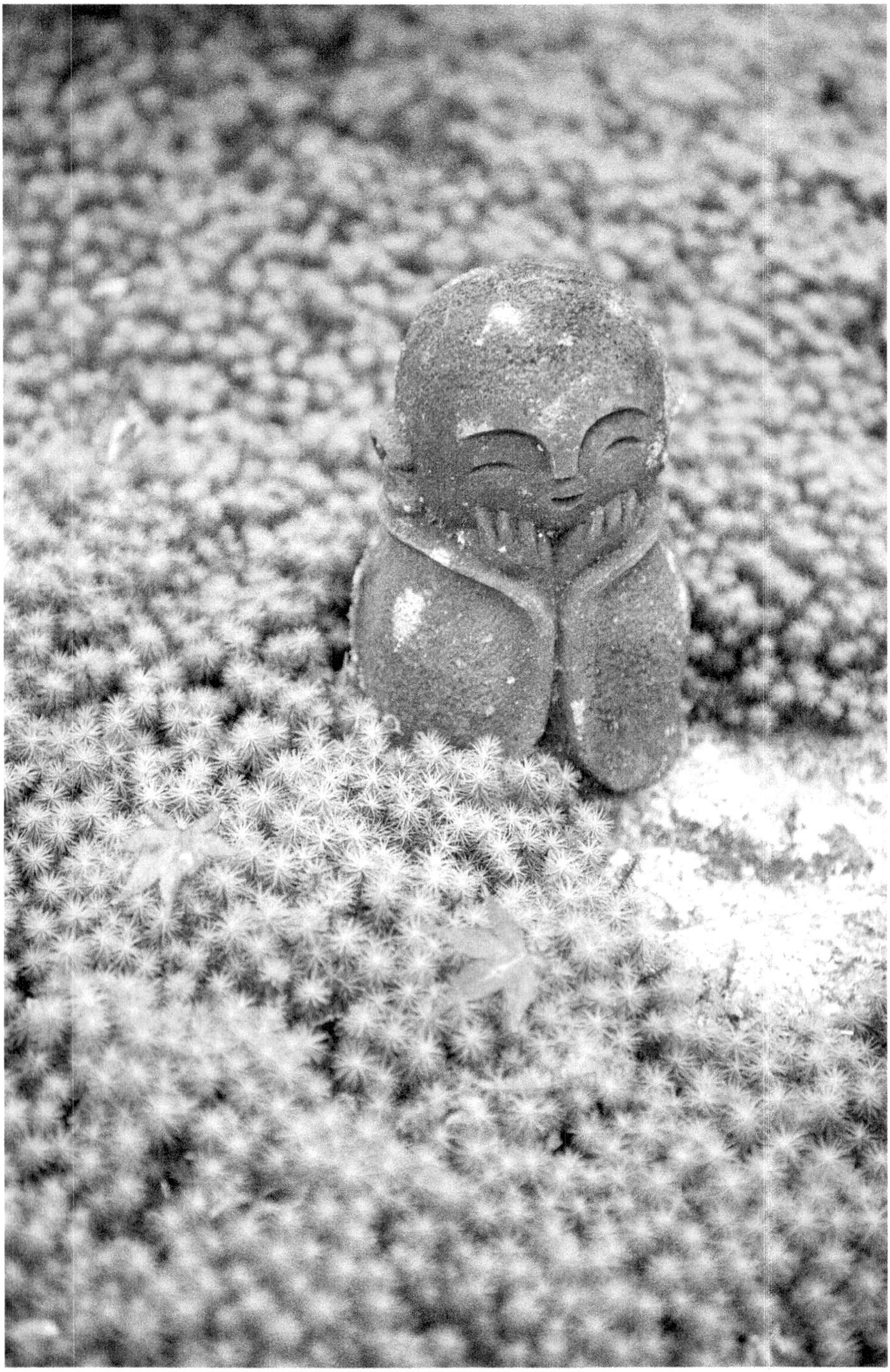

# Kyoto's Nature *versus* My Apiphobia

YUKI YAMAUCHI

Iwao Inagaki (1897–1937), the second son of Lafcadio Hearn, taught English exceedingly well at what is now Kyoto Prefectural Momoyama High School in Fushimi Ward. The teacher was loved by his students, but he suffered from ranidaphobia. According to them, Inagaki fled like a bird on seeing frogs or even craft items designed to look like the small amphibians.

My phobia—which I suppose is not as serious as Inagaki's—is not about frogs but rather about bees and wasps. An Osakaite, I have been oppressed by apiphobia for more than half of my 31 years, since I was almost attacked by a number of stingers during a calligraphy class when I was about 10 years old.

I have two strong memories of Kyoto's nature. One is related to the seaside, before I came to be repulsed by aposematic flying insects. On summer weekends, my family often went surfing or bodyboarding in the sea off Wakayama Prefecture and occasionally other prefectures. We prefer seas to mountains, though our family name includes *yama* (mountains). Such a recreation once led us to Kotobiki Beach on the Tango Peninsula, the northernmost area of Kyoto Prefecture. I had much fun strolling on the beach, which is noted for a wide swath of *nakisuna* (whistling sand). At that time, the sea was not so violent for novices in marine sports, so I could enjoy bodyboarding to the fullest.

My other memory is about mountains, which have always been part of my life in some way. My father drives us to a cemetery in Kyoto's Fushimi Ward three times a year to visit my paternal grandparents' grave (my grandfather passed away before I was born, while my grandmother left this world about a decade ago). The hilly place is surrounded by greenery and therefore visitors are likely to come across a bee or a wasp. Our regular visit there is a chance for us to leave Osaka's urban jungle and walk beside an abundance of well-tended trees and bushes. However, the possibility of encountering stingers makes me so tense that I can find the cemetery's nature beautiful only when we are about to leave for home.

In spite of my phobia, I made up my mind to go to Kyoto's Sanzen-in Temple in the rural area of Ohara around the beginning of March, 2015. At the time, I was intrigued by artworks and statues depicting Amida Buddha. The season allowed me to escape from the din of urban life for a few hours without being bothered by stingers, so I was mentally relaxed enough to take photos.

I spent a good time strolling in the temple precincts—what a wonderful experience it was, to see tiny *jizo* statues standing sporadically on the rough mossy ground with their hands together in prayer. The surrounding neighborhood also gave me a glimpse of what old Japan's shopping arcades used to look like. To be honest, this pleasant time would not have been spoiled even if I had encountered buzzing pollinators.

Time flew by as my senses were comfortably immersed in Ohara's countryside atmosphere, and yet I finally had to take a bus going back to downtown Kyoto. I vaguely remember something like a wasp flying fairly close to the bus stop where a few people, including me, were waiting. Nonetheless, I was not as terrified by the bug as usual. Instead, I felt that insects must be happy to live in such a place, unlike those we happen to see in an urban jungle. My thought was rooted in the work of my favorite Anglo-Irish writer Lord Dunsany, who admired nature and its wonder throughout his entire life and showed his respect for nature in his works.

Unfortunately, my feelings at the out-of-the-way place faded into a part of my past as quickly as the bus took us away. I may be exaggerating, but the vehicle seemed to speed as if it had been a roller coaster on roadways.

Lately, my insect fears have been replaced with tireless vigilance against what the whole world has been suffering from in recent years (I believe we all are too tired of seeing, hearing, or uttering the word).

When the viral risk is low again, I would love to be exposed to Kyoto's nature, which my senses have forgotten for nearly half a decade. I hope to revisit Sanzen-in and Kotobiki Beach, and also go to the former town of Miyama in the city of Nantan for the first time to see quaint houses with thatched roofs, like the ones sheltering many Japanese people in olden times.

Thanks to what I enjoyed at Sanzen-in and its vicinity, Kyoto's nature is something to which I would like to become closer, so that I can temporarily overcome my apiphobia.

⁂

**Yuki Yamauchi**, born in 1991, is an Osaka-based writer and translator. He worked for *The Japan Times* as an event writer from 2015 to 2020. He currently works at a cram school in Osaka, and has self-published several books in Japanese on English-language literature, his favorite writers being Lord Dunsany and F. W. Bain. He likes to visit Kyoto Prefectural Library and, especially in autumn, the Gion Kaikan hall to watch Gion Odori.

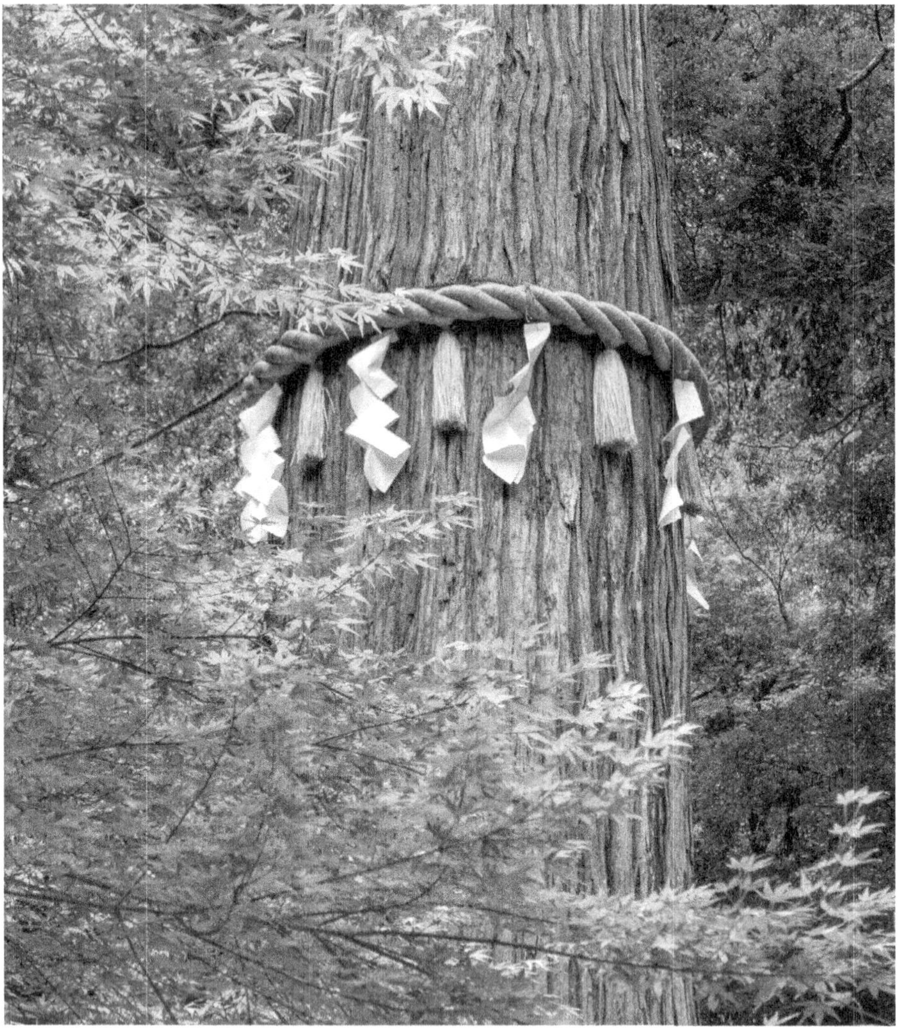

APPENDIX

# *Photographs*

A diversity of photographs captures the people, places and experiences revealed in the fifth Writers in Kyoto Anthology. The copyright holders of each image are indicated hereafter:

| | |
|---|---|
| Shutterstock | cover, 42, 48, 58, 78, 117, 138, 162 |
| Stephen Mansfield | x |
| Rebecca Otowa | 6 |
| John Einarsen | 14, 16, 17 |
| Everett Kennedy Brown | 20 |
| iStockphoto | 29, 47, 145, 161 |
| Elaine Lies | 30 |
| Ted Taylor | 36 |
| firstocean@photo-ac.com | 64 |
| Jann Williams | 70 |
| Shuichiro Kobori | 86 |
| Karen Lee Tawarayama | 94 |
| Ken Rodgers | 102 |
| Rick Elizaga | 105 |
| Kirsty Kawano | 106 |
| Ed Levinson | 110, 166, A-2 |
| Malcolm Ledger | 118 |
| Mayumi Kawaharada | 128 |
| Robert Weis | 132, 146 |
| Alessandro deBellegarde | 156 |

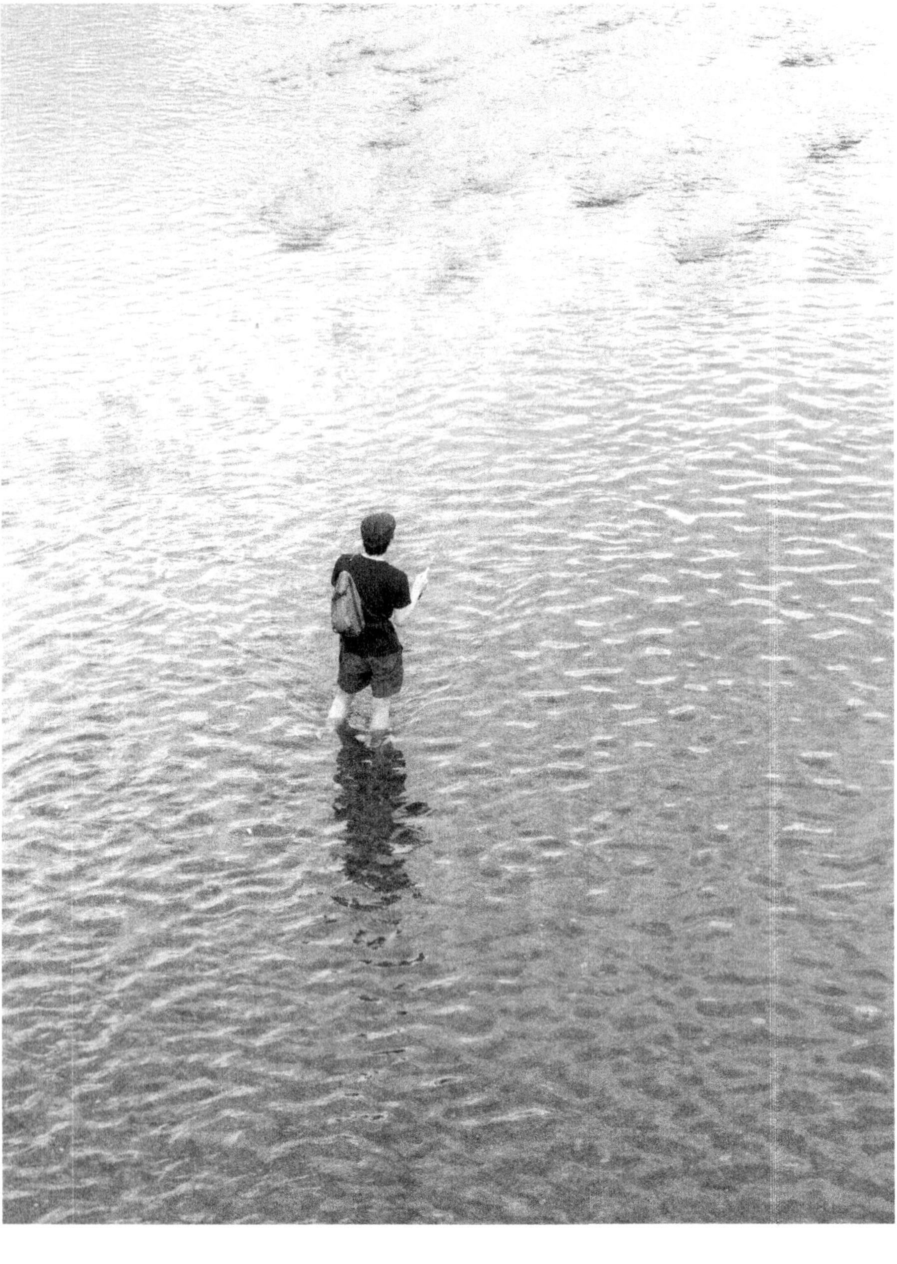

Printed in Great Britain
by Amazon